From Ascot to Tobruk and Back

A True Story of Courage
Humour and Mateship

Mark Thomas o'neill

Copyright © 2013 Mark O'Neill
Red Hand Publications
All rights reserved.

All photos copyright reserved.
Cover Photos and art work design: Mark O'Neill
Maps: Mark O'Neill

ISBN: 0992319803
ISBN 13: 9780992319809

ACKNOWLEDGEMENTS

I would like to thank especially Gordon Wallace and Jack Anning for sharing their memories with me. Also John Mackenzie –Smith and members of the 2/15th Battalion remembrance club for keeping the stories alive, Peter Stanley for his encouragement and various authors, who have supplied background information. Special thanks to the staff at the John Oxley Library, Peter Dunn for Oz@War, and Bill Rudd for POW, as their work contributed to the story. I would also like to thank my family, for their love and support.

TABLE OF CONTENTS

Prologue vii
Introduction x

Chapter 1.   "Ascot" 1
Chapter 2.   Fun and Games 10
Chapter 3.   The 2/15th and Tobruk 26
Chapter 4.   The War Comes to Ascot 57
Chapter 5.   The Endless Patrol, Palestine & Syria 70
Chapter 6.   El Alamein and the Battle for Pee Wee Ridge 78
Chapter 7.   POW 93
Chapter 8.   "The Real Invasion" 106
Chapter 9.   Kangaroo Point 116
Chapter 10. The Battle of Brisbane 127
Chapter 11. Keep The War Quiet: Eagle Farm 135
Chapter 12. Peace and Prosperity 143

Conclusion: The End of An Era 158
Bibliography: Texts 163
Appendix 1. 167
About the Author 175

Appendix 2. Letter 1................................... 176

Appendix 2. Extract from Letter Letter 2 179

Notes to Chapters...................................... 181

PROLOGUE

Ascot and Tobruk you might ask, which Ascot and how are they connected? Two well known places, on opposite sides of the world, what's the story here? Well, my father was born in Brisbane in 1922 and grew up at in Dobson St. Ascot. The old house stayed in the family and my Dad's widowed sister lived there. I used to visit as a child when my father would drop us kids off with Aunty Glad to be baby sat while he and mum went out to dinner.

Keith O'Neill, Dobson St. Ascot aprox.1926 O'Neill Collection

So from an early age I was familiar with the house that Dad had grown up in, just off Racecourse Road. There were still a couple of stables out the back and various bits of old junk lying about. This was the early 1960's.

It was a fun place to stay, a bit dark inside with very old furniture such as a hall stand with a green glass walking stick hanging on a hook. Later in life Aunty Glad passed away and the house was sold but we always felt a connection to the place, often taking a turn down Dodson St. just to check it out. It has only been as an adult that I have gradually pieced together the tale of the people who lived there.

Jim, Way back in the dark days. Photo O'Neill Collection

Equally mysterious for me was a person called Jim. A man my father was in awe of. I never met him as he died shortly after I was born, but occasionally I would hear stories about "Jim". He was a "Tobruk Rat", a title spoken of with some reverence by my Dad. Well liked, he acquired two nick names and being of Lebanese descent he had a deep olive complexion which earned him the moniker "Darkey Jim". The locals around Ascot called him this.

"They only had a pint of water a day to drink" and "they stank like pole cats" my Dad would say. This sounded pretty bad to a ten year old, and what was a "Pole cat" anyway? However the word Tobruk was planted firmly in my brain. The Old Man was a great storyteller and much later in life I was fortunate enough to record his tales of early Ascot, the "time of the Americans", Jim going to Tobruk and fighting the Desert Fox; another mystery.

The lives people led in those days were so different to what I had grown up with and is now even more different to the lifestyles and attitudes of today. They say "History is another country, they do things differently there." That certainly is true in this case. At a military writers' workshop, I was told "authors want to write more than readers want to read." Taking this advice I have tried to keep a lid on the detail, as there is an almost endless amount of information out there. Some interesting topics have been skated over but the reader is able to track down other material is they are interested.

INTRODUCTION

I began this story, set in Brisbane and Tobruk, after conversations I'd had with my Dad when he was in his late seventies and early eighties. The two main characters' lives were shaped by the trials and tribulations of the 1920's to 40's. Jim Sedawie and Keith O'Neill lived through the depression of the 1930's and the momentous events of World War 2. Quite a few men who roamed the countryside looking for work during the depression, were soon dodging "Panzers" in North Africa. Keith was too young to enlist so he remained in Brisbane but Jim went to North Africa and did not return for four years.

Ascot has been an historic part of Brisbane since the arrival of the first English explorers. The O'Neill clan came out from Ireland in the 1800's, not long after the founding of Brisbane and at the time of the convict colony. John Thomas O'Neill, my grandfather, whom I never met, was born in Ennis, County Clare. The region is a very beautiful part of south west Ireland that was badly affected by the potato famines of the early 1800's and by the oppression of the English. Many fled to America and Australia. My grandparents had a difficult life bringing up a family in the Depression but surprisingly they owned a camera and there exists photos dating right back to the 1920's. The Irish are known for their story-telling and weaving this double story together has been quite a journey for me, I hope you find *From Ascot to Tobruk and Back* as rewarding as I have.

"Way back in the dark days" was an expression my Dad would use when describing his early childhood in Ascot. These were the days of the horse and cart, blacksmiths on the corner, penny farthing push bikes and a young Keith O'Neill earning two shillings and six pence a week. It's a way of life long forgotten.

Keith at the wheel & Tommy Martin at the Blacksmith's Shop approx 1928. Photo O'Neill Collection

Keith would go on to see great changes and prosperity in the post war years after the privations of his youth. However, Jim Sedawie faced terrible hardship fighting in North Africa and also as a POW. Their friendship and lives however, display true mate-ship over many years and across many miles at a time when a letter from home or from the battle front meant you were OK and still alive. Every day was a struggle and thoughts of home, sweethearts and parents were the only things able to keep you sane in a world gone mad.

Born in 1922, Keith grew up on the "poor side of the tracks". He was just a kid when Jim came to live at Ascot. Jim was born in 1903 and Keith in 1922; eighteen years difference. They were great mates but it was like a big brother relationship. Keith who was an only son, idolised Jim and Jim kept an eye on Keith. They were tough times with a lot of men out of work or underemployed. People roamed the countryside looking for a few days work wherever it could be found. However tough times, made for great characters who took up the challenges of the 30's and 40's.

These characters worked hard all day and enjoyed a beer with their mates in the "Men only" public bars. Women were allowed in the "Lounge Bar" and it was not until the 1970's that these laws were changed. The world of the 1920's 30's and 40's has disappeared almost without trace. This was a vivid and colourful society with distinctly Australian characters who often spoke with a funny turn of phrase, such as "he's been around since Adam had shorts" and "don't scratch your head - you'll get splinters." (see Appendix 1). Society was unaffected by the invasions of modern technology and the contemporary aggravations that assault the senses today.

In this era, few people had telephones or cars, horses and carts were still on the streets, there were no TVs, no internet or satellites, no mass media or terrorist threats. People still experienced their lives directly, not mediated through some technological device, like today. All men and women wore hats and most went to church on Sundays having no doubt what it was to be an Australian. There were very few people of other European nationalities and virtually no one of Asian descent although there was a small population of Chinese people who had a temple at Breakfast Creek. It is still there today. The indigenous people of Brisbane were all but invisible non citizens, without a vote or a place in the community.

Ascot and it's surrounding districts was an historically significant part of Brisbane from the earliest of times. Just around the corner is the famous Breakfast Creek Hotel where you can still get a XXXX beer off the wooden keg in the Public Bar. It is named after the adjoining Breakfast Creek, which flows into the Brisbane River and is where the first white explorer, John Oxley, had breakfast and met the original inhabitants, the indigenous Turrubal People.

Ascot and the adjoining suburbs of Hamilton and Eagle Farm form part of the backdrop to our story, while in the Middle East and

Tobruk, the dramatic events are told from Jim's point of view. His letters from the front, with their descriptions of battle and the soldier's life, told of his longing for home and how much he missed his adopted family life in Ascot. Both characters are caught up in the events of war in their different ways. Jim recounts in one of his letters, (Appendix 1) "this is making an old man of me" and he is a different person on his return to Ascot. Keith however is still a young man after the war and "makes a go of it" as they say, becoming a successful business man.

Society in the Depression era of Brisbane was strongly influenced by Victorian English values. You were either a Protestant or a Catholic, and mixed marriages were frowned upon. There was also a deep and widespread gap between rich and poor as a result of the Depression. Brisbane at that time viewed the British Empire as the height of civilisation and protector of her dominions. This proved to be a false hope when Singapore suddenly fell to the Japanese in 1942.

The Australian Government of the time dreaded another war and supported Neville Chamberlain the English Prime Minister in his efforts to avoid conflict. Australia was still recovering from the First World War and the loss of life of it's young men. The prospect of being involved in another war on the other side of the world was unthinkable. However this was not to be. A sense of dread filled the nation as our Prime Minister Robert Menzies declared it was his "melancholy duty" to bring Australia into World War 2 in support of England and the Empire.

Keith O'Neill was 17 when war broke out. Streetwise from having to do odd jobs from an early age, he was a young man of physical prowess, social skills and a thirst for success. He joined the Civil Defence Corp.- the VDC - and recalled marching up and down the playing field at the Ascot State School with broom sticks in 1939. Working at the Kangaroo Point ship yard and the Eagle Farm military air field, he put in long hard hours contributing to the war effort. Seeing first-hand the impact of the American presence in Brisbane, he was an eye witness to the many surprising events of the time.

Jim "Pee Wee" Sedawie enlisted in the 2/15th battalion, AIF, on June 7th 1940. This battalion was raised solely from Queensland and comprised mostly of men from the bush. The 2/15th became part of the famous 9th Division which went to North Africa and took part in the epic Siege of Tobruk. He spent the second half of the war in POW camps and after leaving for the Middle East. His letters, photos and Keith's family photos and stories of Ascot in the 1930's and 40's give a unique insight in to the lifestyle, courage and mateship shared by the people who lived through these times. The facts are by turn hilarious and tragic. After the war Jim returned to Ascot and the two mates continued their great friendship and all manner of escapades.

Keith recalls, "The first I heard of Jim he was breaking in horses at St. George. He must have come to Brisbane for something to do with race horses. My Father was a horse trainer who worked in the stables at Ascot. There were stables in our back yard and next door. Jim was Lebanese and had come from Melbourne where the rest of his family lived. He was like my big brother, I don't know why he lived with us but he was a great carpenter. Did you see the pigeon cage he built me? He also built-in the verandah on the front of our house, that's where he used to sleep."

After 1945 Keith and Jim continued where they had left off, working at the Cold Stores, setting up a fish run, being founding members of the Hamilton Football Club and having a "ton of fun" as Keith would say. The events of the 1940's would change Brisbane, the economy gradually improved and life was to become different in ways the people could not have imagined. When the American military machine took over Brisbane in 1941 it was like an invasion, only a friendly one. The citizens were in awe and had to adapt to having tens of thousands of foreign nationals permeating every part of their lives. It was American military power that prevented the Japanese from reaching the shores of Australia. If they had landed, my parents would have been on the receiving end of a hostile invasion. I once asked my mother, who was twelve in 1941, what she would have felt if the Japanese had invaded. Freezing at the idea, it was a thought she did not wish to contemplate,

Australians at the time were all too familiar with stories of Japanese atrocities in China.

In December 1941 Australia's Prime Minister John Curtin made his famous speech about how Australia looked to America without any concerns for historical alliances with Britain, as our survival depended upon it. Some thought it was panicky but Curtin feared an invasion that could only be stopped by the Americans. Arriving just before Christmas 1941, they were welcomed as saviours by the people of Brisbane. Thousands lined the banks of the river as the US fleet sailed in, anchoring at Brett's Wharf in Hamilton. They had just been diverted from the Philippines to avoid superior Japanese forces.

Although the locals' worst fears did not materialise, their lives were turned upside down by having to deal with the privations of rationing, social upheaval, long working hours and the loss of many loved ones. However, it soon became apparent that the American presence in Brisbane would have positive effects and bringing the city into the Twentieth Century. New energy, technology and ways of seeing the world were all positive aspects to the social changes wrought in the 1940's. Apart from some conflict between high spirited servicemen and women and the loss of innocence of some young folk, Brisbane found a new self image and became more outward looking, embracing new technologies and social attitudes. The immediate post war years were difficult with continued rationing and shortages however, by the end of the 1940's Australia was growing strongly and the "baby boomer" era was about to begin.

I began this story after conversations I had with my Dad when he was in his late seventies and early eighties. It was during this time he gave me his prized possessions - Jim's letters and photos from the war. Our story springs from their relationship and those original documents. Wider references fill out the big picture of what was happening in the world at large. Brisbane was small city on the edge of the British Empire and before World War 2 was very much a British Dominion both politically and economically. Although we had begun to establish our own identity through bush culture, Federation and the achievements of our soldiers in World War 1, many Australians regarded themselves as British and looked to the "Mother Country" for guidance on the world stage. The advent of World War 2 was to change all that.

CHAPTER ONE

"ASCOT"

When John Thomas O'Neill, my grandfather, Keith's father, arrived in Brisbane, aa boy of ten from County Clare, the passage of time had all but erased any traces of the original inhabitants and the abundant forests, from the minds of the Brisbane people.

John Oxley, arrived at the junction of the Brisbane River and "Breakfast Creek on morning in 1823. He found a scene of natural beauty, "the country of the finest description of Brush woodland on which grew Timber of great magnitude; of various Species, some of which were unknown to us, amongst others, a magnificent Species of pine was in great abundance."[1]

Ascot and the adjoining suburbs of Hamilton, Breakfast Creek and Eagle Farm were some of the first areas to be settled by the English. They formed a significant part of the early penal colony and had been the scene of some conflict between settlers and aborigines. Early records paint an idyllic picture of the landscape. The original residents had lived for thousands of years in relative peace and natural beauty. There was an abundance of food resources which allowed them time to undertake their many cultural and spiritual activities.

Corroborees, the gathering of tribes for dancing and celebration, took place frequently and the area hosted a vibrant social life based on family and spiritual values. Hundreds would gather at the present site of the Brisbane Exhibition Grounds for singing and dancing. Family groups would come from outer districts to exchange goods and learn new dances and stories.

"They understood and appreciated their heritage and knew what they had lost, when driven from their land." said Tom Petrie, the famous Australian explorer and friend of the aboriginals.

"To them it was a real pleasure getting their food. They were so light-hearted and gay. Nothing troubled them. They had no bills to meet or wages to pay and there were no missionaries in those days to make them think how bad they were. Whatever their faults, I could not have been treated better." He said.[2]

"During the convict period at Moreton Bay a depot for female convicts was established at Eagle Farm, and the track to the depot crossed Breakfast Creek at a bridge (1836) near the creek's mouth. The Breakfast Creek flats were useful farmland, and beyond there a German mission station (1888) was positioned on the Sandgate Road at Nundah."[3]

The brutal convict colony that replaced indigenous society eventually grew into a self-sufficient town and then gradually evolved into the modern city that is Brisbane today. Indeed we are a young culture in a very ancient land. It was only 190 years ago that John Oxley sailed up the river looking for a suitable site for a convict settlement when to his astonishment he, his diary records that he met the English speaking inhabitants: Messrs Pamplett and Finnegan, two white escapees.

"We rounded Point Skirmish about 5 o'clock and observed a number of natives running along the beach towards the vessel, the foremost much lighter in colour than the rest. We were to the last degree astonished when he came abreast of the vessel and hailed us in good English." The lost convicts had been living with natives around Bribie Island since they had almost perished at sea. On December 2nd 1823, Oxley and Sterling, with Finnegan as a somewhat reluctant guide, entered the river and sailed upstream as far as present-day Goodna. Early European explorers were unanimously amazed at the sheer natural beauty of the river and its surrounds. In 1829 the English explorer Alan Cunningham described the locals "The ordinary stature of the Aborigines of Moreton Bay is about six feet, appearing very athletic persons, of unusually muscular limb, and with bodies, (much scarified) in exceedingly good case."[4]

In that December of 1823 John Oxley noted the scenery at Hamilton, "Rich flats and fine timber land, peculiarly beautiful, the finest soil, and timber of great magnitude". At Breakfast Creek he reported "Fine open grazing country."

Another explorer Hodgkinson in 1841 described it thus, "The country in the vicinity of the Brisbane River is variegated brush of exuberant richness, clear alluvial plains of the greatest fertility and good grassy forest land."[5]

In his historic work, "The Greatest Estate on Earth, How Aborigines Made Australia", Bill Gammage documents from the earliest eye-witness accounts, the conditions of the land and how the Aborigines maintained the country. This was the condition of the land upon which the suburbs of Ascot, Hamilton and Eagle Farm were established.

The area known as Ascot is located between Breakfast Creek and Eagle Farm. In the early history of white settlement this area was mostly under cultivation as recorded by various sources including Tom Petrie, who was at the time the fourth son of the first engineer of the convict settlement. The book of his "Reminiscences", as recorded by his daughter, paints a very colourful picture of what the local inhabitants of Ascot and Hamilton were doing during colonisation and how the settlers and Aborigines interacted.

"When my father employed the blacks they were always kind and considerate to him. They are naturally affectionate people, and he with a good and kindly disposition, and a sense of fun – for the blacks do so enjoy a joke – was very popular with them all".[6]

The following conversation between Tom Petrie and Dalaipi, a local aboriginal elder in the mid 1800's, gives an insight into the origins of white settlement in Eagle Farm.

"Why did not the white man stop in his own country and not come here to hunt us about like a lot of kangaroo? If they had kept to his own land we would not have killed him."

"No that is true Dalaipi, you see the white man likes to go and find new country and bring bullocks and horses and grow potatoes and corn and you get plenty to eat."

"No fear, they won't give us anything, they are too greedy. They put corn and potatoes in our land that they took from us at Eagle Farm a long time ago, to tempt us when we we're hungry. There were several shot there for stealing corn. ... The white fellow stole the ground, and I don't see any harm in taking a few cobs of corn or a dilly of potatoes when you are hungry."[7]

There were camping grounds around the Breakfast Creek area and the explorers Oxley and Cunningham met members of the clan at the mouth of the Breakfast Creek in 1824. This area just outside the Ascot suburban boundary was known by the Turrubal people as Yowoggerra, meaning Corroboree Place. In 1858 two Aborigines, Dalinkua and Dalpie, from the Breakfast Creek area, wrote letters to the Moreton Bay Courier protesting the treatment their people received at the hands of the white settlers.

Tom Petrie lived in a house on the river where Creek Street joins the river. At the time the areas of Kangaroo Point, South Brisbane and New farm were all under cultivation, "the rest was all bush and swarmed with aborigines."[8]

Ascot was acquired from the Crown in 1855 by James Sutherland and was made into a pastoral lease. The present Sutherland Avenue runs the length of the leafy suburb about half a kilometre from the race track.

Keith's father John O'Neill was born in 1886 and came out to Australia, "in a boat when he was ten", as he recalls. His father,

Micheal, my great grandfather was a boot maker in Ennis, County Claire. It follows that John arrived at Ascot about 1896. They made their home in Seymore Road Ascot a few streets away from where Dad grew up. The details of the early O'Neill's of Ascot have disappeared into the mists of time.

The penal colony had been established in 1824, ninety eight years before Keith O'Neill was born. In 1839 the last convicts arrived in Brisbane and in 1842 free settlement was declared. Brisbane quickly developed into a prosperous colony. Farming flourished and a fresh water stream was discovered at the place where the Hamilton Hotel now stands.

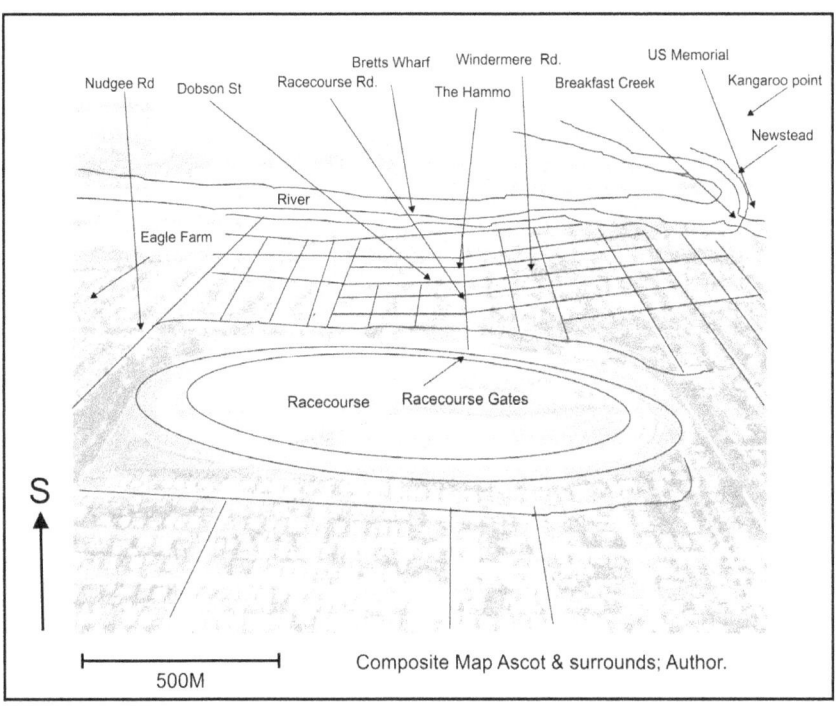

Composite Map Ascot & surrounds; Author.

Eagle Farm racecourse was established in 1863 and was named "Ascot" as a comical reference to the track of the same name in England. It was here that the American military established "Camp Ascot" in 1941. Several hundred thousand service-men camped there on the way to the front. In the late 1890's and early 1900's the larger leases of the district began to be broken up into smaller allotments for housing. The elevated sections of the suburb became much sought-after places to live and continue to be some of the most expensive real estate in Brisbane to this day.

Eagle Farm is the suburb next to Ascot and it became an American air force base for the pacific war in 1941. Keith worked there during the war and it has now become the Brisbane Airport. I still remember sitting on Dad's knee and steering the Ford Customline along the dirt roads behind the airport not far from where I grew up at Toombul. In those days it was open bush and grass land with a few wooden and tin sheds. The Wool Stores were a classic set of old timber warehouses along Nudgee Road and there were probably still a few eagles about at the time. Now the area is covered with airport related industries.

The district of Ascot and Hamilton is neatly divided by Racecourse Road, which extends from the intersection with Kingsford-Smith Drive along the river to the gates of the racecourse. Keith and Jim lived in Dobson St which is a short walk from the racecourse. The horse-drawn tram-car that passed the Hamilton Hotel, in each direction, was eventually made electric and extended to the raceway gates and then beyond to Clayfield and Eagle Farm. The trams of Brisbane, although held in great affection by the people, were discontinued in 1969. On the last day Dad took us boys to the Clayfield terminus and we rode all the way to Bulimba where there were many people waiting to get on. Because no one was getting off they had to wait, and we left without them to go back to Clayfield. The crowds waved as we passed through the Gabba.

Keith was a good mate of Billy Brett, the man responsible for building the Hamilton Wharves and creating the commercial centre based on shipping and transport. The Hamilton "Pub" on the corner of Racecourse Road and Kingsford-Smith Drive was the Old Man's favourite "watering hole' as it was known.

The Second Hamilton Hotel Photo O'Neill Collection

The "Hammo", named after an early settler, had a reputation for being a bit of a rough place in the early days with docks across the street and a cast of colourful characters from all parts, partaking in refreshments.

The present hotel is part of what is now regarded as a well-to-do suburb, along with Ascot. There have always been expensive homes on the hills overlooking the city and with river views, but since the 1990's with the redevelopment of the Brett's wharf into restaurants and apartment blocks, the character of the area has completely changed.

The old weatherboard house Keith grew up in has been removed to make way for shops. Many of the district's original "Queenslander" wooden houses have been pulled down and replaced with commercial developments and town houses. However, a walk down some of the streets off Racecourse Road will reveal the street scapes the Old Man would have been familiar with. In fact, in his seventies he lived in Jackson Street and used to walk to the shops sometimes bumping into people he had not seen for fifty years. It was a happy closing of a circle for him.

Today, at the junction of Breakfast Creek and the Brisbane River, on the Hamilton Reach, there is the Australian-American memorial dedicated by Lyndon B Johnson in 1951. An impressive 12 metre stone column topped by an eagle, below which is a plaque bearing the inscription,

"THEY PASSED THIS WAY"

> *"This monument was erected by the people of Queensland, in grateful memory of the contribution made by the people of the United States of America to the defence of Australia during the 1939-45 war. Long may it stand as a symbol of unity between our two nations."*

Significantly it refers to "the defence of Australia" suggesting that Australia was under threat. It seems this little patch of ground was destined to have a significant place in the history of Brisbane. During the war it was the sight of an anti-aircraft battery because of the clear view over the city and the ships at Brett's Wharf about 1000 metres away. In fact there were guns mounted all around the city in those days. Brett's Wharf was an easy walk from where Keith lived in a house built in the 1900s. He and his mates swam in the river and played on the pylons as the wharf was being built. During Christmas 1941 the American fleet tied up to the wharf. Imagine the surprise of those who had played there only a few years earlier.

**Boys on Bretts Wharf Pile Driver.
Aprox. 1932, Photo O'Neill Collection**

CHAPTER TWO

FUN AND GAMES

Jim "Pee Wee" Sedawie, or "Darkey Jim" as he was sometimes called, was born in Melbourne in 1903. He was from a family of Lebanese immigrants and he wandered the countryside looking for work ending up in Brisbane. Leaving home must have been hard for him but it seems that Keith's family at Ascot took him in during the Depression. He was a horse breaker and roustabout, who came in from St. George in Western Queensland. Jim was a great carpenter and "jack of all trades". At first he lived in the stables in the back yard but later he built-in the verandah of the house and that was where he slept from then on.

The Pigeon Cage 1943. O'Neill Collection

The Old Man loved Jim, especially for the pigeon cage he built for him when he was about ten or twelve. The photo of them on the roof of the cage, and other photos from that time record a seemingly distant past. Keith was seven years old when Wall Street crashed in 1929 at the beginning of the Great Depression.

His dad Tom was often out of work and young Keith sometimes heard them talking about how they were short of money. However, Christmas was always a big "doo" with bonbons and plum pudding with "zacs" (sixpences) and "tray bits" (threepenny bits) in it. Mum must have made some sacrifices to spend that sort of money but as far as I can remember, there were never any presents to or from anyone."

The O'Neills were not the only ones doing it tough. Descriptions from the history of Brisbane paint a picture of economic decline and social dislocation.

"In 1926 falling wool and mineral prices pushed Queensland into recession. The situation worsened in 1929 with the collapse of world stock markets. As the Australian economy plunged into crisis, the official national rate of unemployment reached 23 per cent in 1930 and rose to 28 per cent a year later."[1]

"The impact of the Great Depression on Brisbane was widespread. In 1933 the city accounted for 31 per cent of the State's population of which 55 per cent were registered relief workers. The itinerant unemployed congregated in camps and hostels across the city."[2]

Keith's father John, was one of this "vast army". I remember Keith saying how his father had only two days work a week and sometimes none. Your reputation was important and a good reference was a handy possession. This one is from the Brisbane City Council Engineer's Dept. dated 6th February 1937, two years before the war and when Keith was fifteen:

"This is to certify that the bearer, Mr. T.J. O'Neill was working under me for the Greater Brisbane City Council for about two years.

I always found him a good worker, sober, honest and reliable. (signed) F.J. Hoekey, District Overseer, Hamilton Ward."

At fifteen a young boy is able to see what is going on in his family and the lack of work and money made a big impression on Keith. This seems to be where he developed his drive to work hard to make ends meet. He was nothing if not energetic. Collective memories of these times are fading now. Gone are the days when Australians would keep a piece of string, or fold wrapping paper to be used at some future date. My parents, Grandparents and Aunties would never throw anything out if it had the remotest chance of being used again. Hoarding was a survival instinct that was born out of the depression and reinforced by rationing and shortages during the war. My generation, the so called "baby boomers" - those born after the war - are the last generation to have had this drummed into them. Present day teenagers don't have any concept of this and are conditioned to throw stuff out all the time and think nothing of it. Our forbears would be shocked to see the waste of today.

Childhood memories instilled in my Dad a desire to help his parents make ends meet and created a lifelong sense of reward for effort. After the war during the 1950's and 60's when he was earning big money, he kept a perspective that eschewed conspicuous wealth. Although owning a beautiful house he refused requests to buy a Mercedes Benz 280se which was a significant status symbol in those days. He always stuck to his Fords. Invited to join Tattersals Club or "Tatts" as it was called he declined. Better for him was the more down to earth and local Lions Club where he spent some time contributing to community projects.

In the days before cars, most people used horse and carts for transport and there was a blacksmith's shop a few doors down, in Beatrice Terrace. His dad was a sometime horse trainer and Ascot was at the centre of the racing industry in Brisbane, as it still is today. Although surrounded by horses Keith was not keen on them. He was once kicked in the head when he was a toddler and he would never get on a horse after that.

Leaving school at 13 and a half, not long after participating in a wild mud fight that splattered the newly whitewashed toilet block, he had to do odd jobs to keep the family afloat. It was during these formative years that he became friends with Jim and developed a talent for fun, mischief and money making schemes. His best mate was Tommy Martin and with a group of friends they made up games that cost nothing and yielded great laughs and life skills. Tricks such as trapping sparrows for tuppence each to pay the electricity bill and walking to the Hamilton pub before catching a tram to save a penny.

Stories from the Depression era portray a way of life far removed from the suburban life of the 21st Century. Hardship is something of a perception; the family had stresses, but just as it is today, it is relationships that make you happy and your response to circumstances that makes the difference between surviving and thriving. Being poor was no impediment to having fun and making do. These stories were recorded when the old man was about seventy five. He had a great memory for detail and looked back with fondness on these times, which we might regard as difficult but were filled fun and laughter as kids are not usually aware of the stresses of their parents.

The earliest stories are from when he was about five and playing with Tommy Martin at the blacksmiths shop in Beatrice Terrace a short walk from home. He used to love turning the handle on the forge to heat the metal. They would run about and play in the streets and all over the neighborhood, with no fear and little concern for parental supervision. At about age ten he got a push bike and his world got bigger. This is what he got up to:

"Did I tell you about my favourite pigeon? Well I saved up 3 shillings and six pence and rode my bike into the Roma Street markets about 9 kilometers away. I said to the man "I want to buy those two pigeons." On the way back when I was nearly home, I got anxious and undid the string on the box just to have a look. *Whoosh*, out went one! I bellowed and cried. "What am I going to do?" Mum said "Go back and ask him if you can have it back, the pigeon will go back there." Well the next day I went back and asked the man. He said "Oh you can have a look, if you can find him you can have him." There were hundreds of pigeons in cages!"

The Speed Wobbles", was a favourite story of mine and I heard it many times over the years. Ascot had some steep hills and one of the local kids' favourite pastimes was to make billy carts and ride at breakneck speeds. Windemere Road is a particularly long and steep hill that ends in a T junction at Racecourse Road. This mad cap episode is from when the boys were about 14:

"Tommy Martin and I used to race our billycarts or trolleys down Windemere Road and try to make the turn into Racecourse Road. This was no easy task because by the time you got to Riverview Terrace Road, half way down you had picked up a lot of speed. Tommy Martins' cart only had rope as a steering wheel but I had invented the idea of winding rope around a broom stick and connecting the ropes to the wheels. The other end had a wheel stuck on. This was a more advanced version of the Billycart. It also had coil springs at the back to make the ride smoother. Anyhow, this day I started just up the hill from Lancaster Road and off we went. We both started to pick up speed and I was in the lead. The problem was with the new idea of the coil springs. They developed a speed wobble! Well wouldn't you know it? Here I am flying down Windemere Road, as far over to the right as I can to make the turn, when a tram starts to come down Racecourse Rd. I've got the speed wobbles and the stick mounted on the side as a break is wearing out and not slowing me down. I've got to decide whether to crash into the gutter or try and make the turn and avoid the tram. I fly round the bend, leaning out to one side with my hand on the brake and the other hand on the wheel. This bloke in the tram sees me coming, alerts the driver and I narrowly escape by flying past the nose of the tram. Well wouldn't you know the commotion this near miss caused! I just managed to duck down a side street and run like hell. I don't know how Tommy Martin got away, but I was sure they would have killed me if they had caught me."

In those days there were not as many people in the district and most people knew everyone in the neighborhood. Backyards were bigger and the streets were largely empty, especially at night. It was safe to wander about and have some fun at other's expense.

"We used to play "knockems". Mum would say "Homework done?"

"Yes", was the dubious reply. The other mothers and fathers wouldn't even ask: "where you *goin*?" Anyway Jackie MacKenzie's house had about eight steps and the Council wouldn't mow the footpath, there were weeds growing that bloody high! Well OK we would sneak up to the verandah rail with a piece of string and hang a big dog bone through the railings. We would hide the string out to the footpath and we would hide behind a bush. We'd pull the string and the bone would knock on the verandah boards. Knock Knock, someone would come out and look around then go back in. We would knock again and they would come out. This continued till they caught on and went mad at us. We would then go down to another house. Another game we used to play was in truck tyres. We would hop inside a big truck tyre, one at each end of the street. Our mates would bowl the tyres as fast as they could towards each other so that they would collide head on. The first to fall out of the tyre was the loser."

"In those early days we used to go down to Gibson Island for picnics and fishing. We thought nothing of walking long distances in those days before cars were common. The river bank was covered with mangroves, with beautiful wide sandy beaches in some places as well as creeks and tidal flats. It was an untouched paradise for us kids. We would catch fish and play in the mud. In the early thirties there was a kind of fun park at Gibson

Gibson Island 1930's Photo, O'Neill Collection

Island. Dad and Mum would take us down. They had stalls to play knockems. This was a favourite Sunday outing." Today Gibson Island is the site of an oil refinery and an industrial zone.

Keith was a mad keen photographer. His parents had a camera and took lots of photos. He eventually got his own camera and used to always carry it with him in the car. It came in handy many times for recording traffic accidents and rare events. His first camera was a box brownie. He and Jim became camera experts and Jim took one to the war. This little story is about how he got his first camera in about 1932.

"I got my first camera but saving up cards from Capstan cigarettes. I saved up 29 cards and so I had a choice, six new tennis balls, sporting gear or a camera." "What will I get? Mum said, "Tennis balls are no good as there's no tennis court, what about a camera, you gotta buy stuff to put in it though? So we sent away for it and one day it turned up. "We've got to get some film - what's film?" I said. The camera took 120 film which we got from the chemist. I was about 10 years old at the time." This was the beginning of a lifelong habit of taking a camera everywhere. He kept taking photos till he was in his eighties.

The old bloke had a great fascination with locks from an early age. He collected locks and keys and instead of going straight home from school would walk past O'Brien Locksmiths in the valley. Becoming friendly with the owner, he would be shown show the latest locks and he would have a go at unpicking them. The early ones were easy to unpick but eventually they became too difficult. As a teenager a favourite past time was to sneak out at night and walk in to the Valley which was about three kilometres away. Here he would go around the big warehouses and unpick the locks just for the challenge. Never taking anything he would always left the place locked up and nobody was any the wiser. This fascination extended to always having a security box at home. When I was a kid there was a welded steel box bolted to the floor at the bottom of the old man's cupboard. Cash and coin from the business was kept there. In the early 1960's when 50cent coins had more than 50 cents worth of silver, there was a heavy canvas bag with quite a few that had been collected and saved for a "rainy day".

From an early age Keith saved money from his many odd jobs and eventually bought a Malvern Star push bike. He and his mates went everywhere and thought nothing of riding for hours out to the bush, camping for a few days and riding back. Toorbul, is about an hours drive from Ascot on present day roads in a modern car and it was a great fishing spot. The family would sometimes drive out and hire boat. Keith takes up the story:

"In those days the road from the highway to the water was just a sand track. One time the car broke down and we had to walk to the highway and catch a lift back to town. There were no worries about the car. No one would pinch it in those days. A few days later Dad went back with the part and retrieved the car. It was about this time that for some reason Dad gave away my dog Toby to some cousins who lived out that way. I couldn't believe that they had done this, so I got on my bike and rode out there. It started to get dark and I got a bit scared but I kept going. When I got there didn't they get a hell of a surprise !

"What are you doing here?" "I've come to get my dog." I said, "and I'm not leaving until I get him back". They drove me back the next day, with the dog."

Glasshouse Trip, Photo O'Neill Collection

17

On one occasion when the Old Man was about fourteen he and his mates rode their push bikes to the Glasshouse Mountains, a distance of some seventy kilometres on today's roads which have been greatly improved since the 1930's. They camped on a farmers land with his permission and set up their "Indian" tents. They had what were called "pea rifles" or air guns. A lot of people had a general mania for shooting things in those days. The old man told me that they had dislodged a large boulder from the face of the mountain they were camped on. It rolled down the hill and smashed several trees on the way. "We were bloody lucky it didn't hit the farmer's house or his cows." After several days they rode back. This sounds a bit far-fetched but here are the photos to prove it.

Leaving school at thirteen and a half after year seven must have been tough. 1935 was in the depth of the depression and the O'Neills were struggling, but somehow Keith was able to find work and bring some money in. The surprising thing was that he was able to get quite a few jobs over the next few years and before long he was earning a man's pay by the age of sixteen.

Keith recalls: "My first job was in Fish Lane at South Brisbane, opposite the current Queensland Museum. I had just left school at 13 and a half. My Mum used to go to the races with a friend who said she could get me a job. It was working for an old bloke who used to recycle the glass out of old windows. My job was to clean the glass with acid. I remember him saying to wash my hands a lot, no gloves mind you. Anyway the second day I was splashing acid on the glass when the man from the Chinese laundry next door came running in. %@#$!! He said. Well I told the man I was leaving. I didn't like that job."

"My second job was as a delivery boy for a photographic printer whose office was in Elizabeth St. in the city. They were called Roberts and Russell, a family business. The boss was Mr. Roberts and his brother and son worked there as well. Anyway, they used to print lots of posters and ads for cars and I would deliver them to Austral Motors in the Valley at Barry Parade. I would go like hell, no traffic in those days, mostly horse and carts and this is how I got interested in cars. I used to have all the sample pictures on my wall at home. I then got the idea to get a new bike so I asked Mum who said "well you're getting this money, all you need is a deposit and you can pay it off." I was getting 2 shillings and sixpence a week, later it rose to 17 shillings and sixpence and so I got a new Malvern Star with three speed gears!"

"Another job was at the saw mill at Union Box and Timber company, Newstead. The factory was located on the corner of Montpelier Road on the left hand side going out of town, opposite was Brown and Broads the timber merchant, just near the gas works. When the train was coming they used to wave a red flag and a man would walk across the road. I was roustabout for a couple of days then they put me on tailing out on one of the saws. We started off at about fourteen years old but at about sixteen they would automatically put you off to save costs and get in another crew. It was disappointing. We would get 22 shillings and sixpence a week which was good money and they might keep you on if one of other others retired. It was hard work, and they didn't have any forklifts."

**Union Box & Timber, Keith second from right back row.
Photo O'Neill Collection**

"In the days before fridges, we had a Mawson Ice Chest. Everyone needed ice and it had to be replaced every few days. The engineer who drove the big refrigeration unit for the cold stores got to know us. He used to say we could go in and get as much ice as we liked as long as we told the engineer we were in there so we didn't get locked in. I took a bag with me and dropped the block to break it to take home. I was telling Mrs. Crow and Mrs. Stamfield about this and Dad said "why don't you take a cart down". So he built me a trolley and i took a hammer with me to break the blocks.

I was getting all this ice and Mrs. Stamford said "let me give you threepence for that block of ice." "No, it's all right" I said. But then Mrs. Trout, Mrs. Martin and the Ellisons who all had heaps of kids, wanted me to get ice for them and they all paid me for it. For some reason their own kids didn't want to go down and get it. This was becoming a good business, I was getting threepence for the blocks and going down each day after school. So I told Dad I was going to build a bigger cart. He said if that was the case then I had better get some bigger and better wheels. I had a look at the dump, found the materials and built the cart. I've got the photo of it with my dog Toby sitting up in it. It was a big box and I would load it up. The reason the engineer said we could have all that ice is because by the time it was loaded in the wagons to get back to the farm, it would all be melted. I used to put three of these big blocks in the cart."

"I had to break the blocks to fit them in the Mawson Ice Chest. It had a lid in the top and a compartment about 18 inches long where the ice went. The ice would gradually melt and the water had to go somewhere. Well it was my job to empty the dish underneath the chest every night before I'd go to bed.

Well some nights I'd forget and mum would go out to the kitchen in the morning and there'd be water all over the floor. Dad would say "You didn't empty that ice chest !" I got jack of getting these lectures. I'd remember a lot of times but sometimes I'd forget. So one day when they were at the races and the brain box was *workin*, I thought to myself "I gotta get *outta* this somehow." You see the Dobson Street house was a foot off the ground. I crawled under there and surveyed the position. I thought that under the floor there might have been concrete or something, but no, just pine, ha ha! In those days they didn't have plastic funnels but Dad had a brace and bit. You get the idea, I went upstairs moved the Mawson ice chest and drilled a hole in the floor. They had tin funnels in those days so I went to Dads' shed - he had just about every bloody thing there and there was a tin funnel. I put it in place and the melted ice dripped right into the funnel. Well I thought, *whoopee doo,* you little beaut I'll never have to empty it again.

But you know what's going to happen don't you? Well pluck a figure out of the air, three or four days later, maybe a week I was asked, "Have you empted that thing" "It's right" I'd say. I never said I'd emptied it, just that it was right! Everything was going fine but for some reason Dad had to get under the house, might have been a Leaking water pipe - I don't know. He spots the funnel and there are millions of ants. They couldn't understand up top where all the ants were coming from. Oh boy! Where did ya get that funnel? Oh dear oh dear ! That was the Mawson Ice Chest."

As you might have gathered Keith was a lively character with a good eye for mischief, a fun time and a nose for making money.

"Did I tell you about the first time I played two up? It was in a deserted shop. It's still there I think, just off Beatrice Terrace, in Napier St or one of those streets. They told me and that one of the blokes who was playing the game said, "Listen, there's a bloody dice game on. (two up is the same as dice except you've just got H's & T's on the dice). And he said it just not far from your place, I'll take you there if you like? "Now *muggins* me had never been there before. In those days, when you went to the two up schools you'd give a dud name if you were caught. Didn't occur to me see, so there was I having a go. There would have been fifty of us, two deep round the ring. When, CRASH! It turns out what had happened, there were four coppers at the back door, one with a sledge hammer and he knocked it off it's hinges. There was one copper at each window and two at the front door. We had a look-out and he was supposed to be *lookin* out, but he went to sleep. He was in a utility and they sneaked up on him, and one copper, they told us this later, grabbed him by the throat and said, "Now don't open your mouth or I'll choke *ya*." and he held on to him. So there was no warning and round the back was Brian Davies who turned out to be assistant Police Commissioner. He was a young fella at the time, and it was him who swung the sledge hammer. We were all caught like rats in a trap. No one got away. We were all lined up to be officially processed. So you all join in the queue and by this time they had gone through ten or fifteen and they ran out of handcuffs. So they rang up the Hamilton police to bring some more handcuffs. It was coming up to me and they were all giving fancy pants names. Well I knew one of the coppers and I thought that if I give a fancy pants name, he's *gunna* say, "He's not John Cyril Thomas - that's the name I'd invented afterwards. So muggins me said William Keith O'Neill 14 Dobson St. Ascot. In the paper the next day, every Tom, Dick and Harry was there, they used to put lists in the paper. John Arthur Brown and all these fancy pants names and there was I, Keith O'Neill, 14 Dobson St. Ascot - and they all said, "Ah you been *playin* two up !" It didn't worry me. They got the lot of us and they had to use one pair of handcuffs for two, there was such a mob."

"Not long after this I got my license. I had been driving for about two years on and off so by the time I went for my test I knew what to do. The local sergeant and I went for a drive around Ascot. No traffic lights in those days and no traffic jams. He wrote out the license at the Hamilton Police station and soon after this I got a part time job as a chauffeur for R.M Gow the big grocery merchants in Turbot Street. I was just 17 and I drove a new Cadillac. You should have seen it. I'd pull up with old Mrs. Gow and her sister in front of T.C. Burns in the valley and oh ! you couldn't get near it, people *gawkin* at this bloody car. It was the only one in Queensland. It had belonged to Fred Green at Eagers and he had it brought in specially imported. It had huge running boards and that was the last year running boards were used. It was a 1938 model that weighed two ton and was nineteen feet six inches long and six feet nine inches wide. I was seventeen at the time and this was when I got my first speeding ticket."

Keith's Mum and Dad must have been proud of him. How he talked his way into this job is a mystery, being just 17 he had just gotten his license. Thus began a lifelong love affair with cars and trucks of all kinds.

RM Gow's car and Chauffer, Photo O'Neill Collection

By the time he had developed his business after the war he had owned a dozen vehicles and was an expert self-taught mechanic. The chauffeur job was in 1939 and Jim was working at the Cold Stores at Hamilton, not far from Ascot. Keith joined him there and it was hard work. Keith takes up the story:

"Cold Stores ! That was a favourite one". Jim had asked "Why don't you come with me and get a real job." So I went. It was daily labour, they wouldn't know in the morning how many wagons there would be so you would wait. When the train arrived at 8.20 they might say Ok you, you, you etc., maybe eight men. If you didn't get on you could wait till the next train came at ten o'clock, we would play cards while we waited. When I got on the man didn't ask me my age he just said "you". But you got a man's pay, for a day of man's work. I was 16 at the time. It was good money too, we used to unload the 56 pound boxes of butter, that's a half a hundred weight or 25 kg. They were packed in pine boxes, ever seen them? very sturdily built, thin but strong. They used to stack them seven high and then when they were "stacking back" they would stack them eight high. I could stack them seven high but when they were stacking them eight high, *littlies* like me had to stand on one at the bottom to stack the last one.

They were in the train wagons and we would pick them up and put them on rollers, push them to the inside on a conveyor who would stick them in the freezer. Everybody liked to get the freezer job, because you got 16 bob a day if you worked outside and I think you got 22 shillings and sixpence if you were inside. One day a Union man shows up, "What's he do" I asked. "You have to have a union ticket to work here." He said, but I didn't know what a union ticket was.

"The boss was an old bloke named Jack Bodley, a Scotsman, very tough but he was fair. Tough but fair. So this day it's a few minutes after starting time and Jack Bodley comes around and I haven't started. "What are you doing Keith?" "Err Mr. Bodley that man said I can't start because I don't have a union ticket." "Who told you that?" "That man there."

"I'm telling you to get in there and start if you want a job." So off I went! They got into a heated argument, a hell of a bloody *barney*. Jim said the next day, "This union business, he's likely to call a strike and then none of us will have a job." So I begrudgingly gave this bastard ten bob. What do they do for you and I'll bet he gets a cut."

One day Jim saved a man's life. There was lot of yelling going on and men standing around. "What's happening?" "There's a burst ammonia pipe and a man is stuck inside the cold room." He would have died in there as the ambulance would have had to come from Anne Street. Jim put a cloth over his face went in and pulled him out." It seems Jim had displayed physical courage when those about him had frozen.

"Early in the piece we would have two pairs of pants and three pairs of socks and three sweaters on and a beanie on your head. The union must have got to them, because later on, the cold stores had to supply you with proper clothes and a proper apron. It was hard work, you would be tired at the end of the day. You used to ride your push bike to work and back, which wasn't that far. Not long after this the war started and I wanted a job where you worked every day."

In fact the war had been going for some months and Jim must have been discussing with the family what he was going to do. It was not long after this he joined the army. Keith was seventeen at the time too young to join but old enough to know what was happening. He felt the loss of his mate going away and the frustration of not being able to join him. What was he to do? Always on the lookout for a better job he became a shipyard worker. But our story now follows Jim's path as he heads into the unknown.

CHAPTER THREE

THE 2/15TH AND TOBRUK

Private James George Sedawie volunteered for service on 07 June 1940 at the Kelvin Grove Barracks. He became a member the 2/15th battalion AIF, which was raised solely from Queensland. Thirty seven years old at the time he was an unmarried truck driver as recorded on his military "Attestation Form". Like an uncle to a lot of the men who were much younger, he became a popular member of the Battalion for his great sense of humour and being always ready to help his mates.

After Australia entered the war in support of Britain on 01 September 1939 a number of battalions were raised. They were named the 2/13th 2/17th and the 2/15th which was intended to echo the original First World War battalion numbers. The 2/15th was commissioned on 01 May 1940 and Colonel Marlan, a regular military officer, was appointed Commanding Officer. The raw material he had to work with was tough and resourceful and full of larrikin spirit. Most of them had grown up riding horses, fixing fences and living out in the bush. They possessed that Australian knack for making do with whatever was at hand. Jim was a typical "Jack of all trades" who fitted into army life with ease and whose bush skills would stand him in good stead for what lay ahead.

They commenced training at Redbank, in Brisbane and were soon posted to garrison duty in Darwin. They sailed out on the

Zealandia in July and had a very colourful time mingling with the locals when they reached Darwin. Coming into contact with the Darwin Mobile Force, who seemed to resent their presence. A few social occasions were attended and more than a few scrapes were had with the local "Redbands" as the Darwin Mobile Force was known and after one particular fight, it was recorded that Colonel Marlan issued them a stern warning. However at a full battalion parade, where there were several black eyes, bandages and Redband souvenirs, he said that "he was proud to see that his men had not disgraced themselves."[1]

**Jim Darwin Photo
O'Neill Collection**

Jim's service record from this time reveals that he was admitted to the Darwin Hospital on 27 July and discharged on the 02 August. It was recorded earlier that back in Brisbane he had been "admonished" for being AWOL in June and had later been fined a Pound (20 shillings) and punished with 14 days detention for being asleep in a tent away from his post. Jim was not a great stickler for Army discipline, although he was apparently quite handy with a pair of barber's scissors, and often cut the men's hair.

On 27 October the men re-boarded the *Zealandia* and sailed back to Brisbane where they enjoyed pre-embarkation leave from 10 November. On Christmas day they caught the train for Sydney and on Boxing Day boarded the *Queen Mary* in Sydney Harbour and sailed in convoy to Colombo. After a brief stopover in Colombo they boarded the Dutch troop ship *Intrapoera* and passed through the Suez Canal at the end of January. They landed at El Kantara on 03 February and saw many interesting sights along the way. The battalion history mentions such sights as a Sudanese Pipe band, "Black as Pitch" of which Jim took a photo, along with other locals. He also photographed the Anzac Memorial from the first war on the Suez Canal.

During their passage through the Suez they were briefly held up by enemy planes dropping magnetic mines over the canal and they had to wait for them to be cleared. When they arrived in El Katana they boarded a troop train to Palestine and finally reached their training camp *Kilo89* near Gaza. It had been about eight months since the battalion was first formed in Brisbane and here they would spend the next few weeks being "hardened" with intensive desert training.

**Barber Shop Darwin 1940,
Photo O'Neill Collection**

The "War in the Desert" as it was called started when the Italian army, based in Libya, invaded British protected Egypt. Mussolini was convinced that Britain was finished and that her surrender to Germany was imminent. Taking advantage of this situation the Italian 10th army advanced meekly into Egypt and stopped just inside the border at Sidi Barini. Here they refuelled and stocked up on food and wine and waited for the counter attack from the British. This soon arrived in the form of the 4th Indian Division and the British 7th Armoured division, who advanced rapidly and captured 20,000 prisoners.

In early December 1940 General Wavell began what he believed would be a short five day raid against the Italian forces in North Africa. This action developed into a full scale campaign as the Italian forces collapsed before the British advance. On 12 December 39,000 Italians had been captured or had surrendered and Bardia had been taken. Tobruk was 90 kilometres to the west and neither Churchill nor Wavell had expected to capture it, however the momentum was such that they advanced to what was 150kms past their original destination. For the White Kangaroos of the 6th Division - Tobruk was in their sights.

General Richard O'Connor quickly pressed the advantage and started to pursue the Italians across North Africa. The Indian division was sent to Ethiopia and was replaced by the Australian 6th Division. They were on board a ship heading for the battle front. After cavorting while on leave in Cape Town, they arrived in time to be in the vanguard of the taking of Bardia on 03 January 1941. They immediately took part in the total routing of the Italian 10th Army. This small force pushed the Italians across Cyrenaica to Benghazi, defeating ten divisions and capturing 130,000 prisoners, 400 tanks, 900 guns and 1000 aircraft for the loss of under 2000 killed or wounded.[1]

In ancient times Tobruk had been a Phoenician colony under the rule of Carthage. A trading post during Greek times, it became a Roman garrison town and later an Italian colonial outpost. This part of North Africa was originally inhabited in Neolithic times from about 8000 BC by the ancestors of the Berber peoples. After the decline of the Roman Empire it became a trading post for rebellious Bedouin tribes, governed by heavy handed Byzantine rulers. Its political status changed hands regularly until by the mid 1400's it had become a part of the Ottoman Empire ruled by Suliman the Great, who presided over a vast kingdom.

Eventually the Ottoman Empire fell apart and was reduced to a democratic Turkey, leaving Tobruk to fend for its self. From the early 1900's Libya was ruled by the Italians and was known as Italian North Africa. One Hundred and fifty thousand Italians migrated there and made up twenty percent of the entire population. They had fought a short war with the Ottomans and turned the town into a fortress. The name Libya was introduced by the Italians in1934 although the modern state of Libya was not declared until 1951.

Tobruk, is the only safe deep water harbour on the coast of North Africa, west of Alexandria and has always been a strategic military asset. Its long history of being fought over was about to be extended. Mussolini tried to invade Egypt after declaring war against England on 10 June 1940. General Graziani complained to his leader that his forces were not equipped for such a venture but was nevertheless ordered to proceed. They had moved tentatively into Egypt and dug in as the British gathered themselves and began the task of forcing them back. Overall the Italians had 236,00 troops in North Africa, while the British had only 100,000 of which only 36,000 were available at the time. They began to be pushed westward out of Egypt and this was when the first Australian forces were deployed in battle.

Tobruk was populated by 27,000 Italian troops who saw it as a key base. However, their fortress was overthrown by the rapidly advancing forces of Generals Wavell and O'Connor. By 20 January Wavells' two Divisions had arrived on its outskirts. The Australian 6th Div went in and it was said by an unknown Australian that "The police in Tel Aviv gave us a better fight than this".[2] The Italian army was smashed and only half of the original troops in North Africa remained. The Italians had been defeated much more quickly than expected and the possibility of a complete rout and the capture of the capital Tripoli was being considered. If they had been given permission to press on to Tripoli, the Italians would have been completely defeated in North Africa and there was doubt as to whether the Germans would have considered it possible or worthwhile to intervene.

However, military strategy and politics clashed and one of Churchill's damaging strategic blunders was foisted upon the Allies. As the North African campaign was proceeding, the Greek army was handing the Italian army a similar defeat in defence of their homeland. These defeats were noticed in Berlin and Hitler considered sending troops to Greece but made the decision to send support to Mussolini in North Africa. At this time Premier Metaxas of Greece had refused several offers of assistance from Churchill on the basis that the presence of British troops in his country would provoke a German response. However in the second week of February Premier Metaxas died suddenly and his place was taken by Alexander Koryzis who then accepted Churchill's offer of help.

The Australian 9th Division, including the 2/15th Battalion and the British 2nd Armoured division were depleted of equipment and resources in order to bolster the campaign in Greece. At the time Churchill's advisers thought it unwise and Anthony Eden his Sectary of State for War, noted in his diary that it was a "Strategic folly".[3] This view was held by all the British leaders in North Africa at the time. In early April 1941 the Australian 6th division was withdrawn from Tobruk and sent to Greece to participate in what both Robert Menzies and the Australian Chief of Defence, General Blamey, considered a very risky exercise which might end in disaster. But Menzies felt that Greece should be supported against German aggression and that the defence of Greece was a "great risk in a good cause".

Churchill regarded it as politically necessary to support the Greeks and so the Aussies and Kiwis were sent. As predicted, the Greek campaign ended in disaster with a hasty retreat to Crete. It fell to the Australian 9th Division, to replace the 6th Division in North Africa. If the Greek campaign had not been undertaken there would have been considerably more strength in North Africa, the routing of the Italians would have been complete and the Germans may not have sent an army to support Mussolini. As it turned out the forces left to confront Rommel were much depleted. At the time the famous Australian poet Kenneth Slessor was a war correspondent and at a later press conference he asked General Blamey, the Chief of Australian Forces if the Australian lives lost in Greece were lost in vain. After several minutes of silence Blamey answered: "That is a difficult question and I am afraid I can't answer it."[4]

The Greek campaign became a serious issue in the Australian press to the extent that the Department of information restricted further coverage. The diversion of troops to Greece had left the North African Theatre undermanned and under equipped. As it turned out The 2/15th battalion were left exposed and caught up in the chaos that was the next period of the North African and Mediterranean campaigns.

On 27 February the 2/15th battalion boarded a train and spent the next few days travelling through Palestine and Egypt en-route to Mersa Matruh on the Mediterranean Coast of Egypt. For some days they travelled in captured Italian trucks through the desert, passing towns on the North African coast, including Sidi Barrani and Bardia. It was at Mersa Brega that they helped to replaced the 6th Division, who had captured the town from the Italians in a famous rout. From Tobruk they travelled to Agedabia, not far from Benghazi. An advance party went forward to Troca which was the British forward defensive line. By 22 March 1941, the battalion had taken up a defensive position at Mersa Brega near Benghazi, this was the most western point the Australians achieved.

The German High Command had been keeping a close eye on these proceedings and had dispatched General Erwin Rommel and a small force to Tripoli in order to support their Italian Allies. They feared being driven out of North Africa completely. Against orders Rommel, although his forces were not at full strength, attacked these allied positions immediately, in order to prevent the British from reinforcing their positions. The Allies fell back to Regima, a position which quickly became threatened, and some headed straight for Egypt. What followed was called sarcastically, the Benghazi Handicap or the Tobruk Derby.

Sgt. Gordon Wallace, a young man at the time, who is now a sprightly ninety one years old, sharp as a tack and with a good memory, has given his time and friendship generously, in helping me piece together this part of the story. As president of the 2/15th Battalion Remembrance Club, he is in demand as a speaker at many military functions. Here he recalls the *Benghazi Handicap*:

"We had no idea Rommel was in North Africa until we came under attack. I was with my Coy. at Mersa Brega when we saw a German fighter plane approaching. He was at about fifty feet and the rear gunner spotted me as they flew over. I had a Bren gun with an anti aircraft mount and a piece of cloth over it to keep the sand out. It was held on by a safety pin. As I struggled to get the pin undone and the cover off, he came down at me firing. His sights must have been set for a longer distance, as the shells went either side of me as he had a go."

Anyway as we got closer to Tobruk we came to a small cross roads with a bloke in a British Field Officer's uniform directing Traffic. He spoke good English and told us to take a side track. We asked why, were we being directed into the desert instead of the coast road to Derna. We noticed that his uniform had a bullet hole in the chest and what appeared to be fresh blood. He was a German; Lt. Parker shot him and we went the other way. It turned out that Colonel Ponath was in there with amour and had captured some of our blokes." They spent the next four years in prison camps so it seems that Gordon and his mates were a bit smarter or luckier than the Generals.

These "blokes" as it turned out were the English Generals Neame and O'Connor who had left Derna at night in their staff car and in the hasty retreat, took a wrong turn and got lost. With them was the 2/15th headquarters company, Col. Marlan and most of their bren gun carriers. Early that next morning they found themselves in the midst of an armoured column, but alas the voices around them were foreign. They were in the middle of the German advance. It is evident that some form of battle took place before the surrender, as

Lt. Col. Marlan recommended Private Rae for the Military Medal, due to his actions under fire. He posted his recommendation from his prisoner of war camp and although it was not awarded at the time, Col. Marlan resubmitted the request after the war and it was eventually awarded in 1950.

The British and Australians were in full retreat which would not stop until they reached Tobruk some 460 kilometres away. It was here they were told that the fortress and harbour must be held at all costs. If Tobruk fell, the way would be open for Rommel to take Alexandria, Cairo, the Suez Canal and the Middle East oil fields.

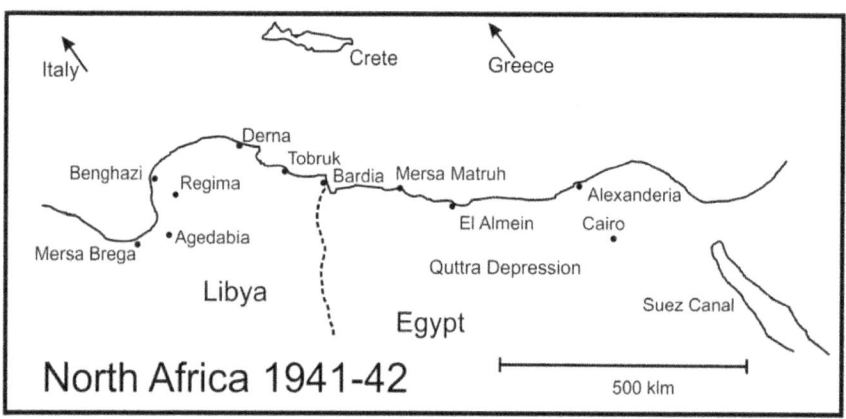

Composite map, Author.

The chaotic retreat of approx 400 klm was a disaster for the Allies. Gordon recalls that the mortar section of the 2/13th battalion used their weapons as makeshift anti-tank weapons on the run back and that at the Barce Pass his section were stuck overnight with no transport until the early hours of the next morning. This was about 07 April 1941. Corporal Fearnside of the 2/13th battalion said this about the arrival in Tobruk:

"By the time we got to Tobruk our nerves were ragged. All the way back from Regima we'd steeled ourselves for the action which never came and every soldier knows that the waiting before the attack is the worst."⁵

The troops had been bombed, strafed and harassed by the Germans but with some protection from the Royal Air force 3ʳᵈ Squadron of Hurricanes. The *Benghazi handicap* was not a day at the races. They arrived in Tobruk exhausted and confused from their first experience of warfare, pulling back at speed with the Germans on their hammer. And frustrated from not having been able to confront their enemy; but they knew that opportunity was not far away.

Jim in A Coy. made it to Tobruk on 10 April and as they took up their defensive positions, were informed that the German attack would probably come at dawn the next day. Rommel attacked Mera Berga in the first week of April 1941, occupied Benghazi on the 7th and began the siege of Tobruk on 11 April. The Allies had to cover seven hundred kilometres in just over a week while being attacked. What a nightmare this must have been for the retreating soldiers in desert conditions with trucks breaking down and being left behind; it was a huge feat of endurance just to make it to Tobruk.

Rommel pushed as hard as his men could go. His attitude was always to attack at speed to keep the opposition off guard in order to make sudden breakthroughs and achieve quick victories. He was expecting the defenders of Tobruk not to have had enough time to prepare their defence.

Rommel was exhibiting all the recklessness and dynamism for which his leadership was renowned. His minders in Berlin were trying to reign him in and he was told by army chief Walter von Brauchitch at the Fuhrer's briefing on 19 March 1941, "that no decisive strike was to be made in North Africa at this point." 5. However Rommel had decided to ignore his superiors and attacked. He subsequently routed the Allies and chased them all the way from Benghazi to Tobruk. Three days before arriving outside Tobruk Rommel wrote to his wife:

"8 April 1941. I have no idea whether the date is right. We've been attacking for days now in the endless desert and have lost all idea of space and time. As you will have seen by the communiqués, things are going very well. I am very well. You need never worry".[6]

These fateful words were written just days before the Easter Battle which was his first attack on Tobruk.

Rommel had arrived outside of Tobruk and immediately ordered one of his best soldiers to attack. General Von Prittwitz charged down the road towards Tobruk at the head of a light armoured column and was killed by anti tank fire. Undeterred, Rommel ordered another unprepared attack, this time leading his troops in a futile attack in an unarmoured open topped staff car.

Rommel was known to act like a Compamy commander rather thana General. This stemmed from his actions during the First World War when, as a Lieutenant, he had led his troops in several famous victories. He had a tendency to lead from the front, act impulsively and leave the logistics of battle to his office staff. Consequently by the time he had reached Tobruk his supply lines were over extended, his supplies low and his troops exhausted. He was also not to know that General Wavell was cleared for "Ultra" intercepts. These were the top secret intelligence reports being generated by the British at Bletchley Park, which had decoded the German "enigma" machine signals. This decoding had alerted Wavell to the reports coming out of Berlin and gave him the advantage of being forewarned of their intentions. However Rommel had the advantage of knowing the Allied intentions. He had information from American broadcasts in a code that the Germans had deciphered.

Rommel was under the impression that the defenders of Tobruk were a disorganised rabble intent on evacuation by ship as soon as possible. In his haste he had severely underestimated the Australians and their intention to make a stand. As it transpired they had just enough time to establish themselves in the Italian trenches prepared some years before. This bit of breathing space gave them a fighting chance against the coming onslaught. Rommel's overall objective was to capture the Suez Canal, however Tobruk was the only viable harbour and supply depot between the western coast of North Africa and Egypt; whoever held Tobruk and the harbour, held the supply lines and thus the upper hand. The Australian and British forces were told in no uncertain terms that Tobruk must be held at all costs.

A meeting was held between General Wavell and Gen. Lavarack in Tobruk on the 08 April 1941. It was agreed that Lavarack would assume command of the Allied Forces in Cyrenaica and that Tobruk must be held till reinforcements could be brought in. Wavell was recorded as saying: "There is nothing between you and Cairo and it may be necessary to hold Tobruk for two months." Australian Major General Leslie Morshead was appointed to command the defence of the Tobruk fortress and his response was: "There'll be no Dunkirk here. If we should have to get out we will fight our way out. There will be no retreat, no surrender."[8]

Morshead

Rommel

Joining other parts of the 9th Division, the 2/15th arrived in Tobruk on 10 April 1941. After their chaotic and draining retreat from Benghazi, they had developed into a cohesive group whose motto, "Cevant Hostes," - let Enemies Beware", was put into action as they took the fight up to the Germans. With the help of the Royal Horse Artillery they were to hold Tobruk against all odds for eight months when the High Command had originally expected the siege to last two months. With less than twenty four hours to prepare, they readied themselves for what they knew was coming.

What was coming was the "Easter Battle", and all hell would break loose as Rommel's elite armoured force tried to smash into Tobruk. All through Belgium, Holland and France, Rommel and his Panzers practised "blitzkrieg" lightning warfare. Unprepared and ill equipped armies and civilians fled in the face of their onslaught and so Rommel was supremely confident in his ability to take Tobruk quickly. He would rush in and the opposition would capitulate. However, he had not anticipated what was in store for his battle hardened veterans. What followed is recorded as the first time the German army was turned back. The Easter Battle was fought in April 1941. Jim Sedawie, a "foot slogger" or infantry man in A Coy. of the 2/15th, was in the front line as the Panzers attacked and confronted the 8th Machine Gun Battalion as they followed the tanks in. Many books have been written about Tobruk and the Easter battle is a famous episode within the overall story but until recently the role of the 2/15th A Coy. in this engagement was not recognised in the official histories and other notable works. In fact, the Australian War Memorial official version had also missed the role of this group of men and it was left to John Mackenzie-Smith whose father fought in the battle, to follow the story and publish the true account.

In April of 2011 at the 2/15th Battalion's Anzac day Dinner I sat with John and he recounted how questions had arisen in his mind about A Coy., the group his father was the leader of on that fateful day. He said:"I asked my father how far away the tanks were; his reply was - about thirty yards."[9]

John told me that this didn't seem to fit with the published accounts and it was from here that he began the research for his book *Tobruk's Easter Battle - The Forgotten Fifteenth's Date with Rommel's Champion*. This account, from original documents and eyewitnesses, shows how A Coy stood their ground when the tanks came through. In some cases the tanks went over their trenches. A Coy engaged the following machine gun battalion and put them to flight. Their leader was Rommels champion, Lt Col. Gustav Ponath who had been awarded the Iron Cross, one of Germany's highest military medals for his exploits in leading the 8th machine Gun battalion in France and Belgium.

The specific instruction of Morshead was to, "let the tanks come through" so as to engage at close range and separate them from their infantry support. It also meant that the British Artillery, tanks and anti-tank guns would be more effective as the Allies could not match the German armour at long range. Although exhausted from their punishing week of chasing the Allied troops across the desert to Tobruk, Rommel insisted on pressing the advantage. Blitzkrieg warfare meant swift penetration of the enemy's defences with tanks and aerial bombardment; "the point of the spear", followed by infantry to capture on the field of battle. The Australians had captured Tobruk quickly against Italian troops who had put up some spirited resistance but Rommel who was within striking distance, was given false intelligence that the Australians were low on morale and were about to evacuate. Nothing could have been further from the truth. The Germans were convinced they could not be beaten; for the Aussies, retreat was not contemplated. Gordon summed up the situation this way: "It was a case of win or be captured or killed. The only option was to win." The defenders of Tobruk were highly motivated, determined to take on the enemy and backed themselves to do the job.

"Ming the Merciless" as Morshead was called, laid his trap and the elite German troops rushed straight into it. Chester Wilmot's map, which was drawn just after the battle and Capt. Greg Smith's map show that Moreshead arranged a funnel for the Germans to advance into. The 2/15th A Coy. were at the head of the funnel and the 2/13th and 2/17th Battalions on front lines either side. The Royal Horse Artillery were placed at the rear behind the 2/15 A Coy. What happened next was described by German tank crews who survived the battle, to be like a "witches cauldron". The co-ordination of the infantry, tanks and artillery as planned by Morshead was executed to perfection. The Germans were caught off guard as the artillery opened fire at point blank range and the Australians ducked down and let the tanks roll over them.

"On the morning of the battle it was estimated that over 25 tanks had massed in front of the A Coy position, being dug in 200yards in front of the artillery's position. The enemy attack was supported by air dive bombing attacks and the noise of battle was intense."[10]

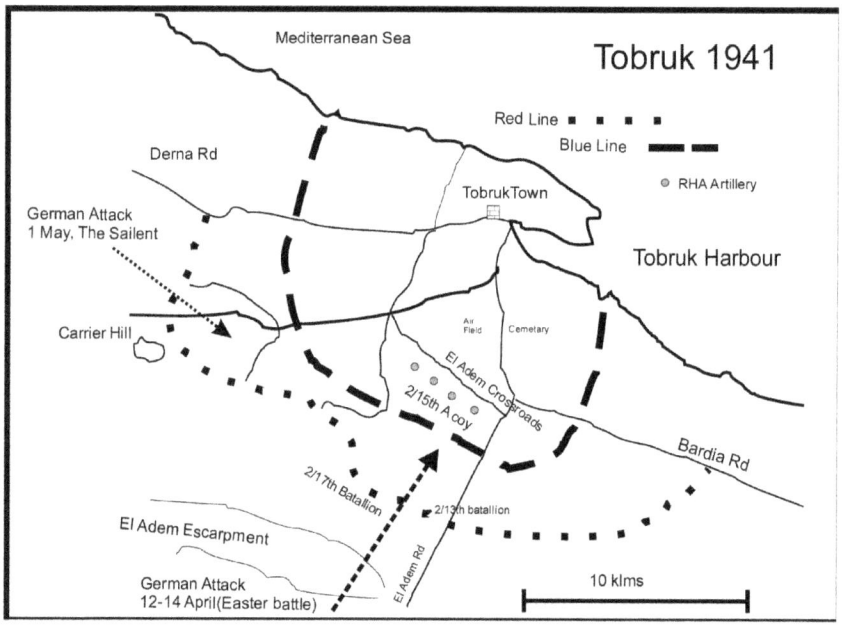

Composite map, Author.

At one point A Coy was about thirty yards away from the tanks and were attempting to fire down their barrels with rifles. Drawing the tanks in had the two fold effect of allowing the British 25 pounders to fire over open sights and separating the tanks from their supporting infantry. The leading tanks tried to smash through the defence while one troop of four British gunners fired more than a hundred rounds per gun in twenty minutes. As the guns were dug in almost to ground level, the tanks could not stop the firing and at one point a massive Mk4 Tank had the turret blown clean off by two shells hitting simultaneously. Still the German tanks took a heavy toll on the British artillery, knocking out several of their guns and killing many of the gun crews. However they fought back heroically, destroying several tanks and managing to turn the rest of them around. As RHA RSM Batten recounted "We were about to fire again when a 75mm shell hit us square on the shield. The gun was knocked out and all the crew, except myself were either killed or wounded. I managed to fire the round that was still in the gun and the tanks turned tail and withdrew. It was a good thing they didn't know we couldn't fire again"[11]

Of the RHA Jack recalls that "We saved each other."

All hell had broken loose, but the allied men in the field of battle were there for each other, looking after their mates and not backing down. The blokes who were there tend to understate their experience, but I can't imagine confronting a tank with a bolt action rifle about two cricket pitches away. The German veterans of French and Polish campaigns were and assumed a victory was theirs for the taking. The Australians were raw recruits, this being their first serious engagement. Leaving their trenches, they advanced over open ground and routed the far more experienced opponent. The Aussies were proud that when called upon, they backed themselves, stuck together and got the job done. Some months after talking with John Mackenzie Smith I met Jack Anning, a veteran of the 2/15th and a member of A Coy, who was good mates with Pee Wee. They were there in the trenches together when the tanks came through. One tank that was hit by shell fire that came right over their heads. Jack said, "We were lucky the Italians had made such good concrete trenches, they were great workers."[12]

Morshead's planned tactic was to separate the infantry from the tanks. The Australians and Royal Horse Artillery were able to implement it to perfection, and it is what happened after that, that got me to start writing. In Pee Wee's August letter from Tobruk, not long after the battle, there is a passage about the death of a German officer and the surrender of the machine gun unit. Pee Wee was a member of the group engaging the enemy in the open which, according to the records was Lt. Yates 7 Platoon. Jim's letter, (full text Appendix 2), from Tobruk dated 17 August 1941, takes up the story and in his own words:

"Every one of their infantry men carry a machine gun of some description while we have 1 to every 7 men, and still we can beat them, they are terrible frightened of our bayonets. ....30 of us took 120 prisoners and they took us by surprise as we were advancing in the open, and they were in trenches, but we never stopped."[13]

Jack recalls: "As the tanks had started to retreat, our job was to stop the infantry getting to the British artillery. They were milling around, they were right up close, on our hammer and we got stuck into them. They went to a tank trap which was about chest deep, there were lots of these about 30- 40 feet long. While there was a bit of a lull and our Sergeant Major Robinson who had the only pair of field glasses, saw them in the tank trap. We thought they were going to hold fast till night and try to infiltrate into Tobruk. Old Greg Smith said: *A Coy. get ready.* We were set to go and we thought we were going out to get twenty five or thirty."

"After the tanks were turned around, the immediate battle field was strewn with burning tanks and planes. The supporting infantry, the German 8th Machine Gun Battalion, left the cover of the tanks and took refuge in a partly dug tank ditch and dispersed into whatever slight depressions they could find. Subsequently Capt. Smith sought permission to send a raiding party out to engage the remaining Germans."[14]

Jack recalls: "They had plenty of fight left in them. We were running low on ammo and they had some wounded. It was a bit of a stalemate."

As Lt Yates' 9 Platoon traversed open ground 800 yards out, they were fired upon by rifles and machine guns. The patrol went to ground and while some kept the enemy's heads down with covering fire, the rest moved to higher ground and out flanked them. Sgt. Long John Cunningham noticed movement in the ditch and sent for reinforcements, and after raking the ditch with Bren gun fire 25 Germans surrendered. However those surrendering were fired upon by their own men, some seventy in number. This brought a response of mortar and Bren gun fire from the Aussies and when the Germans realised they were trapped they surrendered.

Until 2006 the German version of events of what followed was still regarded as the correct story. It fell to John Mackenzie-Smith to put together the details from eyewitness accounts and solve the mystery of this incident. The German second in command refused to surrender to CSM Robinson who was not an Officer, so Lt. Yates took the surrender. It has also been noted that many of the Germans were weeping with frustration as they believed they could not be beaten as their Nazi propaganda had told them. Jack was Yates' bodyguard and was on the spot when this happened. Jack recalls they were ordered to drop their arms and about eight of them held up a piece of white cloth and were being escorted away when the officer and another soldier rushed back to the ditch. Ponath wanted to make sure his men were looked after. Then he went back to the trench and opened fire and made three shots with his pistol. He didn't try to hit anyone, the shots went overhead. But at the same time Yates shot him. Jack and Pee Wee witnessed this, and Pee Wee's account includes Ponath's last words:

"it is just not war with you Australians; the way you keep advancing on us under such heavy machine gun fire."

Comforted by his weeping second in Command, who had asked Yates for permission to be with his dying friend, Lt Col Ponath, who had been awarded the Knights Cross for bravery in previous European campaigns, passed away. It was too humiliating for him to surrender in front of his men and it seems that he committed suicide. Jack remembers clearly the Second in Command and the many Germans crying at the loss their leader.

When he died the 2IC, stood up and gave the most correct salute and clipped his heels like the Germans did. He then spread a red Nazi flag over his body before handing Yates his revolver. He told his men to surrender and they were marched off. On discussing Pee Wee's letter with John and Jack, we agreed that this was an eyewitness account of the events. Many years later John donated the Nazi flag from this day to the Australian War Memorial and it can be seen today in the Tobruk display.

What was it like to be an infantry man, a "foot slogger" in the North African campaign? Pee Wee's letter is vivid and remarkably well written for a man who was an itinerant labourer with little education. I am still amazed every time I read it. Penned during some of the most difficult times of the siege, it recounts all the typical trials and privations suffered by the soldiers. See Appendix 2 for the full transcript.

One of those trials was the regular visits of the German air force, the most feared example of which was the Stuka dive bomber. Although vulnerable to attack by fighters, the Stukas had virtually free reign over Tobruk. Designed to frighten those on the ground, they were fitted with air sirens on their wheel mountings and would scream as they pulled into a near vertical dive. This is what Pee Wee had to say about them in his letter:

"You were asking me about close shaves, well no person is safe in Tobruk no matter where he is as our furthest point from the sea is about seven miles, and what damage their guns cannot do their dive bombers can and believe me, you have no idea how them dive bombers make you get under cover. I wish you were just finishing the boat that was going to bring me back to Aussie, as this place is making an old man of me, all the young fellows are just nervous wrecks, as you have no idea the effect the dive bombers have on us, especially when about 50 or 60 come diving down on you, and if a bomb drops close you go deaf for a week, and each plane carries 5 bombs and then they machine gun us, so you can imagine how our nerves are when they come round 14 or 15 times a day."

Damien Parer was an official Australian camera man stationed in Tobruk. He worked closely with Chester Wilmot. They often observed the action in town and down by the jetty while shooting films, he remarked "For the next hour they were coming over in ones and twos, every ten minutes or so. As the drone of one died away we could hear the next coming in, the greeting of the gun, the rumble of bursting bombs and then the *ack-acks* spasmodic farewell. We thought it was a fairly warm welcome, but for Tobruk it was just an ordinary night. I sat on my backside and waited for these raids. "Stuka parades" the boys call them, and I got some good stuff. The first raid had about 15 planes, the next 30 and the final 50."[15]

Crashed bomber: Tobruk, Photo J. Sedawie, O'Neill Collection.

That's 95 planes in one night. Tobruk was surrounded by German airfields and Rommel had virtually unlimited air resources. At times the air would be thick with planes, high level bombers, Stukas and ME109 fighters.

The original squadron of thirty two British fighters had been reduced to thirteen by the end of April and was finally withdrawn as it would have been suicidal to keep sending them up. They had been the only Allied air cover from Tobruk to Alexandria. They had fought bravely up to this point and had in many cases had significant wins over the German air force. However the defenders of Tobruk were now left without any air cover. Pee Wee said "We just have to take it as it comes. I have known a time when I haven't left my trench for 3 days, only to have a few shots when I could not hear a plane about and we have no air force to protect us."

Rommel threw everything he could at them in the lead up to the next battle. No wonder some of the men were nervous wrecks. However it was also true that direct casualties from bombing were relatively few as the men spent virtually the whole time in their slit trenches, which provided effective cover.

One of Morshead's directives was that the Australians would control no-man's- land, the area between the two front lines. This was achieved through active patrolling; aggressive defence groups, varying in number from half a dozen to sixty, went out at night to terrorise the Germans and Italians as they slept or kept watch in their fox holes. After a time the patrols were equipped with special rubber soled shoes so as to not make a noise and overalls with reinforced elbows and knees for crawling through rough ground and camel bush. One typical episode was when an Australian patrol crawled right up to a German position and tied a piece of cloth to their wire, just to let them know they had been there. What would you think if you were a soldier in that trench?

"Lets Charge the Bastards," typifies the attitude of the Aussies. These words, recounted by Fred Brockel, were spoken by Sgt. R.A. Patrick in the middle of a fighting patrol when he stopped in a ditch with his mate to reload:

"There was a lot of moaning and groaning coming from the German positions, so I think we must have inflicted a lot of casualties on them, I also heard Snowy Roselt, who was badly hit and lay dying calling "Mother of Mercy". I was lying on the left hand side facing the enemy; Lofty was lying next to me in the middle, with Sergeant Patrick on the other side. Lofty said "What do we do now?" I was busy reloading my rifle and was losing as many as I put in my magazine in my haste to reload. Patrick said: "Let's charge the bastards again."

That raid was on the 31 August and was led by Capt. Lance Bode who began with the message; "Come on boys, up and at em." We charged. They swung four machine guns straight on us and a volley of grenades burst in front of us. For a few seconds the dust and flash blinded us but we went on. In the confusion I ran past the machine gun post I was going for and one of those useless *Itie* money box grenades hit my tin hat. The explosion knocked me down but didn't hurt me. As I lay there the fight was going on all around, I could hear *Ities* shouting and screaming and our Tommy guns firing and grenades bursting all around. I rolled over and pitched two grenades into the nearest trench and made a dash for the end machine gun post. I jumped into the pit on top of three Italians, and bayoneted two before my bayonet snapped. I got the third with my revolver as he made for a dug out where there were at least two other men. I let them have most of my magazine. Another Italian jumped into the pit and I shot him too. He didn't have any papers so I took his shoulder badges, jumped up and went for my life."[15]

Pee Wee, who had been on many patrols, was a hardened veteran by this stage. His account of patrolling in his April 1941 letter is as historically significant as it is colourful:

"We have him very frighten at night time because we sneak up on him, at different places and always clean up a few of them, they are that frighten now that they have a searchlight, but that does not stop us and as for the Italians they are the frightenest men I have ever come across. They have watch dogs, and believe me once the dog barks, we can start chasing them but can never catch up to them."

The Australians hold on no-man's-land created a stalemate. They couldn't break out and defeat the Germans, but Rommel was unable to take the fortress. Thrust and counter-attack, with a drawn out war of attrition is was what followed and this is where the Aussies got christened the "Rats".

Lord Haw Haw, whose real name was William Joyce was an English language broadcaster of German propaganda. Early in the siege of Tobruk he made mention of the Australian soldiers being caught like "rats in a trap" and "poor desert rats". This was due to the conditions the solders found themselves fighting in. They lived in trenches in filthy conditions, often with poor rations. The Australians adopted the name with pride becoming "The Rats of Tobruk."

After the Easter Battle, Rommel had found a new respect for the Tobruk Rats. He realised he would have to bring all his forces to bear in a concerted attack if he was to take the garrison. Two weeks after their first defeat, Rommel was ready to strike a decisive blow. Meanwhile, General Paulus, sent from German high command, reviewed operations and approved the new plan, and the 15th Panzer division arrived. On 30 April first the Stukas, then the artillery unleashed their fury on the Australian forward positions around Hill 209. The Germans and Italians came in firing tank shells from 200meters and with flame throwing tanks attacked the forward positions. They blasted a hole in the perimeter defences, used grappling hooks to pull down the wire and followed by infantry, broke through and captured several posts of the 2/24th Battalion. During intense fighting many were captured and killed. However the outcome was inconclusive, and the stalemate continued. Rommel had underestimated the Australians again and had only managed to capture a bugle of territory, the "Salient" as it became known.

A German doctor captured at the time said: "I cannot understand you Australians. In Poland France and Belgium once the tanks got through the soldiers took it for granted that they were beaten. But you are like demons. The tanks break through and your infantry still keeps fighting."[16]

What transpired was six weeks, between early May and mid June, of thrust and counter trust by both sides as they struggled for a decisive advantage, a battle of wills that was won by the Australians against all odds. Rommel was again thwarted in his attempt to capture Tobruk and had to settle for holding "The Salient", the only piece of high ground.

From here he could see over Tobruk and was able to make life difficult for the defenders, but was not able to proceed any further, due to the stout defence and aggressive patrolling by the Australians, often to their great cost. Reinforcements were hard to come by and some Australian Army Service Corps men were drafted into the front line from their jobs as truck drivers cooks and other support crew. Ern Wood recalls:

"I and others were integrated into D Coy. for the next few months. In the process of moving to the Salient, I was moved to another platoon. Corporal Steve Carson was in charge of the section and Lt. Frank Carter was to be platoon commander. I only saw him once and in the darkness when he arrived one night to take up command of the platoon. He went out on patrol and was killed (with others) by a mine explosion."[17]

This part of the siege would drag on for months with the soldiers enduring terrible conditions. Jim's letter gives us some idea.

"Front line troops cannot leave their posts and go for a swim, and I have only been twice in six months. It is dangerous to swim anywhere as the water is full of mines and booby traps and you only have to touch them and they will blow you sky high."

"Dust, heat and flies everywhere, rations are scanty and we are restricted to one water bottle per man per day. There is no water for washing. The best I could do was to use the water I could put into a 2 ounce tobacco tin. With this water I cleaned my teeth first, then shaved with the same water then after that douched my face, eyes and ears. There was no other water."[17]

The food was not much better either consisting of tinned Bully Beef that came out as a slop. The biscuits were hard a rock and had to be soaked overnight to make them edible. Gordon recalls that "We used to pick up small lumps of vegetable, sort of extract made something like a Vita Brit, these were Italian, but we were picking them up, out of the dirt of course, but they had a lot of garlic in them and that added a bit of taste to your bully beef when you made a stew or whatever."[18]

Gordon, who was in B Coy. Recalls: "They would man the trenches on the Red Line for three weeks at a time. In some trenches they were only thirty to forty metres from the German lines. (That's' two cricket pitches or the width of a football field). Both sides rations would have to be brought up in a tank. When the rations arrived and were attempted to be delivered - it would be *on*.'

Australian Trench   **"The Ones We Left Behind"**

Photos J. Sedawie O'Neill Collection

After their stint in the Red line they would go back to work on reinforcing the blue line, the inner defensive ring. Like Jim, Gordon recalls having a pint of water a day for all uses and only getting two swims in six months. When I asked Gordon if he ever thought they wouldn't make it out of Tobruk?

His immediate reply was "No, we never though Rommel could get us out. I don't know why, we just did."

Later he said to me: "I have been thinking about that question you asked me, you know, if I thought Rommel could get us out - and I thought we must have been cheeky bastards, we were only 19, but we never thought we would lose. And when I asked Jack what he thought, he laughed and said more or less the same: 'No

I never gave losing a thought; we must have been cheeky young blokes."

I also asked Gordon if he got used to Tobruk to which I replied: "You just had to. It was a job. You knew you could cop it any time but you didn't think about it. You just got on with it."

Undermanned and under armed compared to the Germans, who had every kind of weapon and all the equipment they needed, the Australians who often had to rely on captured Italian supplies, repeatedly drove them back. Most of their Bren gun carriers were captured in the Benghazi Handicap and their anti tank rifles, which were out of date, would just bounce off a Panzer. Jack once brought down an Italian plane with an Italian machine gun as it came in low over their trench strafing. The Australians held on through will power, unshakeable self belief and excellent leadership. Was it this "never-give-up-attitude" that the Germans had no answer for?

Lack of fresh food and hygiene became a serious problem with medical orderlies treating up to twenty or thirty cases of dysentery per day. The men were very thin and looked emaciated. The slightest scratch would break the skin and desert flies would get on the wound and cause sores.[18]

Chester Wilmot records how some of the Diggers passed their time. Laconic Aussie humour made light of their predicament. This typical exchange was a bit of relief in a harrowing life of tension: "Beer? I haven't had four beers in the last six months". This was from Charlie who was a Queensland miner and he didn't do very well on a water bottle a day. Another digger called Ernie chipped in: I know what I'll do when I get out. I'm going to a pub and am going to have a hot bath and splash the water all over the floor. I'm going to waste it. Then I'll drain out the mud and I'll fill the bath again with clean water and I'll lay there and wallow. And while I am lying there they can bring me iced beer. And when I've had enough of the bath and I've had a feed, I'll just get into bed and they can bring me beer and more beer. I've got a six months thirst. Charlie broke in: "What if you was given the choice of a beer or a bath right now what would you pick?"

"I rather have a bath" said Ernie, "One beer now would only take the dust off my throat. I rather get clean in a decent bath and get on some clean clobber instead of the lousy things you have to live in here day and night till you stink." They all agreed with Ernie, but a cup of tea would have done as we hadn't had one all day. We didn't have a primus and we couldn't light a fire. The enemy hadn't picked up this post and the boys didn't want to give him a trail of smoke on which to lay his machine guns."[19]

While grimly holding on, many deadly patrols were sent out, usually the Italians and Germans came off second best but sometimes the Aussies lost men too. Records show that the Africa Corps was doing it tough as well, with supply lines stretched, food shortages and the same unrelenting desert conditions. Long hours were spent waiting for nightfall, putting up with heat and flies and not knowing when a Australian bayonet was to appear. Gordon recalls early one just morning before dawn he spotted a few a Germans, having a leak and shaking out their blankets. He said to his mate:

"Come and have a look at this." "What are we going to do was his reply?"
"I told him we'll do nothing – we'll wait till tomorrow. Well the next morning we went at them and they didn't know what hit them, poor buggers."

Aggressive patrolling preserved the Australians buffer from the numerically superior German and Italian troops. For months, there were many losses and injuries on both sides as they tried to wear each other down.

We know from Jim's letters that thoughts were often of home. His letter of 14October 1941 when he wrote: "Remember me to Pommy and tell him I expect to have Christmas dinner with him. I thought that I would have left Tobruk 4 or 5 days ago, but I am still here. Things have been pretty hot here these last few nights and there have been a few deadly battles and that may be the reason we have been left here. I am just dying to get out of here so that I could have a dam good feed of fresh meat and eggs and things and have a good hot bath and clean up." (excerpt Appendix 3)

As these "deadly battles" raged Keith was at the Kangaroo Point ship yard building Corvettes for the Australian Navy. He was working hard and earning good money. Receiving letters like this one must have been distressing, knowing his mate was literally in the firing line. Christmas without Jim would have been sad for the O'Neills. And Jim was keen to know what Keith and the family were up to. He asked in his letter: "Well Keith you never told me much about your girl friend, do you think you will be getting married and can you send me a snap of her if you have a spare one, I am just dying to see what she looks like."

In this letter written days before leaving Tobruk and eight months after the start of the siege, Jim seems at his wits end. What was meant to be a two month stint had dragged out and pushed the men to breaking point. The High Command knew they had to be replaced or their health would have been too compromised but in order to get out of Tobruk they had to take their chances getting onto a boat in the harbour. As Jim said: "Keith you asked me about the salt water, well I've drawn you a sketch of Tobruk. We hold the town or what is left of it,

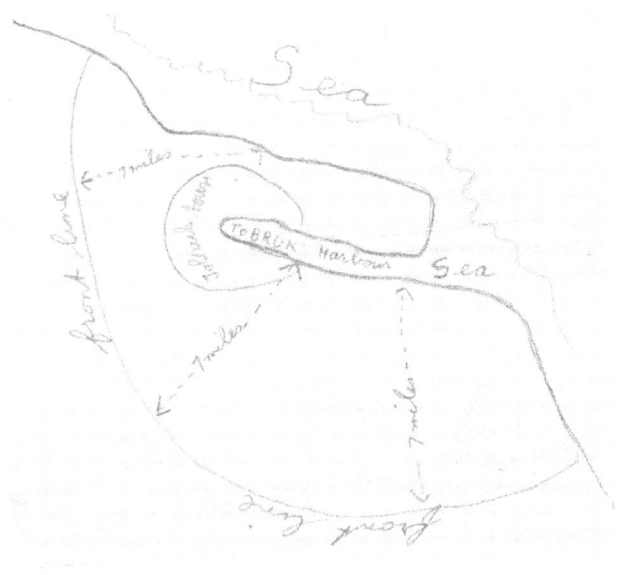

Map of Tobruk, J. Sedawie, 1941, O'Neill Collection

with only a few buildings still standing and the long narrow harbour as you will see by the map I drew you is only about twice as wide as Breakfast Creek; you can nearly throw a stone across it and that's where they get our boats. The boats have to pass close to the Jerries' lines to get into the harbour and we only hold a circle about 7miles out all round"

Jim's hand drawn map, on a scrap of paper shows the layout of the town. The harbour was often the centre of activity and conflict. Leaving was a high risk affair and they were not safe till well clear, as shown by the sinking of the HMS Ladybird. Wilmot and Parer both used to go down and watch the loading and unloading. Many of the ships would come and go at night but this was not always possible.

Tobruk Harbour 1941. Photo Slouch Hat Publications

The HMS Ladybird was a small British gun boat anchored in the harbour. It was repeatedly attacked by Stukas with the crew on board valiantly fighting back. She was hit by several bombs and began burning fiercely. Many of the crew jumped into a burning sea but the gun crew on the front deck kept firing even though their ship was ablaze and had sunk in shallow water.

The 2/15th battalion record below shows that they were shelled constantly till the day they left:
5 days 222 enemy shells on A Coy.
19th: 151 shells
Hand over to 2nd Black Watch 23 Oct
Embarked for Alex (Alexandria) 25 Oct 41.

Finally A and B companies of the 2/15th boarded British navy ships for the trip to Alexandria on 24 October 194. The 2/13th battalion remained in Tobruk until December when the siege was finally lifted.

A letter dated 30 October 1941, which is just before Pee Wee left Tobruk, has a hopeful tone and recounts a meeting with a friend Normie. There is a great photo of the two mates at the Hamilton pub after the war. Normie was Keith's mate Norm Douglas who had enlisted as a dispatch driver.

"Well Keith I must not forget to tell you that I saw Normie yesterday, and wasn't I pleased to see him, he looks terribly well, I woke him up out of his sleep as he had been on night duty, and when he opened his eyes he thought he was still dreaming he could not believe his eyes, I stopped with him for an hour then he came up to my camp with me. God knows when I will see him again. I don't think it will be too long now, it seems impossible for it to carry on at the rate it is going much longer."[22]

As they were driven from their defensive positions to the wharf, German planes were bombing the harbour and British *Ack- Acks* threw up a barrage to keep them off. The ships were protected by the anti aircraft guns which were often an effective deterrent. Rommel did everything he could to close the harbour and cut off Tobruks' supply lines, but in spite of some times heavy losses the ships from Alexandria still made the dangerous run. The feelings of relief upon being out of Tobruk and at sea are hard to imagine and loud coo-eee's were to be heard as the ships pulled away, but they were still not safe until they disembarked in Egypt.

**"British Aircraft Carrier being raided by Nazi DiveBombers".
O'Neill Collection**

They were replaced by the British "Black Watch" as well as South African and Polish soldiers. Within a few days the battalion was transported by a combination of ships trucks and trains to "Hill 69" their base camp in Palestine. The 2/15th Battalion had shown that they were indeed a unit to be feared by the enemy. Their motto "Ceveant Hostes" proved to be no idle threat. A period of relative peace lay ahead for what were now veterans, as they headed to some well earned leave and garrison duty in Syria.

CHAPTER FOUR

THE WAR COMES TO ASCOT

As the siege of Tobruk raged, Germany prepared to invade Russia and the Japanese attacked Pearl Harbor. The American Fleet on it's way to the Philippines was diverted to Brisbane at Christmas time 1941. Soon Japanese forces took control of the Western Pacific. General Douglas MacArthur, the Allied Commander, stationed in the Philippines with his family and staff, had to evacuate secretly. Escaping their island fortress of Corregidor in Manila Bay by PT boat to Mindanao, they flew to Australia, leaving behind the remaining American and Filipino soldiers to their fate.

After briefly establishing headquarters in Melbourne and meeting Australia's leaders, MacArthur, made Brisbane his headquarters for the next stage of Pacific War. He had his office in the AMP building on the corner of Queen and Edward St. between July 1942 and November 1944. The people of sleepy Brisbane were about to be startled by some two million Americans passing their way. Apart from some mixed feelings about their arrival, a Brisbane resident, Mrs. Elizabeth Harland, expressed a popular sentiment: A convoy of American ships sailed up the Brisbane River and a young Brisbane woman stood on the banks of the river watching. Mrs. Harland was recently widowed when her husband of only a few months was shot down over Germany while serving with the Royal Australian Air force. She was not alone with her feeling when saying,

"I remember looking at those ships and the men on them and thinking we had been saved. I thought *Thank God for the Yanks. They were our Saviors.*"[1]

Photo. John Oxley library. State library Qld No.45741

On 22 December 1941 the US Navy Pensacola (Gulf of Mexico) arrived in Brisbane, the river was full of ships. This Us Navy had visited Brisbane with a smaller group of ships in March of that year. They were well received by the locals. However the more recent visit had a much greater sense of urgency as the US had now joined the war on the allies side. All around the river banks were fortified with anti- aircraft guns.

"The Americans marched down Queen Street to the City Hall on Christmas Eve 1941 and this gave the people real hope." (Stan Latham, apprentice engineer.)[2]

Bretts Wharf, was an easy walk from where Keith lived. It became the drop off point for the Americans and a major staging post for allied logistical movement as well as the departure point for heading north to the battle front. Vast amounts of materials and men were unloaded. Seventeen years old at the time, Keith got work unloading equipment on the docks. He worked on unloading machinery and fighter planes in crates. Cranes lowered them onto trucks to be taken to Archerfield airport at first, as this was before Eagle Farm was built. As Keith recalled,

"Anyway, one day we loaded this truck with a whopping big crate that had a fighter plane in it. As the truck approached the gate to go on to Kingsford Smith Drive, it was too wide to get out. An argument started with the American crew and the Bretts man on the gate. This went on for a while when eventually a Yankee Captain came over to have a look and said:

"Get some chains around those gates and get them the hell outta here, there's a war on."

The man from Bretts went mad but it didn't make any difference, they put some chains around the gates, hooked them up to the truck and pulled them out. In those days Brisbane had trams and the loads on these trucks were too high to get under the overhead tram wires so men had to walk in front with poles and hold up the wires so the trucks could get through."[3]

The Wharf adjoins Racecourse Road in Ascot which leads directly to the racecourse gates. American service men would disembark from their transport ships and march down Racecourse Rd, through the gates to their camping ground. One day in 2007 when I was driving past the gates with Keith he mentioned that he had jumped up onto the railway crossing and taken a picture of some marines as they marched through the gates. "Where is that photo?" I asked. "I dunno" was the reply. Sometime later when I was going through a collection of old negatives, I found the one of the marines. "as they marched through. I thought, this is it!" I had it printed and it shows clearly the Racecourse Gates.

The Racecourse Gates, 1941. Photo O'Neill Collection

You were not supposed to take photos of the military activities so there are only a few pictures in the Old Man's collection from this time. As a seventeen year old it must have been an incredible sight to have tens of thousands of Americans marching literally past your front door.

The local paper later recorded: "Since 1942 a total of 2,290,757 American servicemen have passed through Brisbane. Of these, 1407 are buried in cemeteries nearby. About 700 have returned to Queensland to make their home here."[4]

At one point "early in the piece" as Dad would say, Keith and his mate Norm Douglas decided to join the army. This is the Norm mentioned in Pee Wee's letter from Tobruk. He was the son of a butcher, who had his shop around the corner in Racecourse Road, which is still there today. Norm had just bought a new "Don R" BSA motor bike. Together they went to the Enogerra Army camp and waited to see a sergeant. As the story goes, Norm got straight in as a dispatch rider and Keith went for his truck license.

"Well we got in this truck and I hadn't driven a truck very much. The sergeant asked if I knew how to double the clutch. Well I pretended I did, but it soon became obvious that I couldn't drive a truck and you should have heard the noise when I tried to change gears. GRRRRRRRR. Holy bloody hell, what a racket. "That's OK", he said after about ten minutes, "Let's go back."

Alert to what was happening in the world, Keith was convinced the Americans were the only thing stopping the Japanese from invading Australia, as he said many times:

"We only had pop guns, if they had wanted to come here there was nothing we could have done. We had a crystal radio set Jim made out of a big cigar box, a piece of wire and a crystal and if you fiddled around with it you could hear the news. Every Sunday night on 4BC Dr. Goddard would come on and he would always finish with: "And remember ladies and gentlemen, 5000 planes for the defense of Australia." Dr. Goddard had been involved in the war in China, where the Japanese were torturing the Chinese. Terrible atrocities, I'm not going to tell you. Well I thought I would see if I could get into the Thursday Island garrison. I was gunna fight the bloody Japanese, Bloody pop guns is all we had, this was just before the war. I tried to join up but they wouldn't have me, under weight or under age I think."

In fact Keith's "Mobilization Attestation Form" from this episode records that on the 06 February 1941 he tried to join the Thursday Island Garrison by putting his age up saying he was born in 1921 instead of 1922. One week before this he had received a letter from the RAAF telling him to report in for an interview as a trainee mechanic.

"I thought that if they wouldn't take me I'll join the air force. I went in to Creek Street but they were only taking top class men, you had to be fit. A couple of weeks later I got the reply: "your services will not be required, we'll let you know. Thank you."

Later on in the war Keith applied for the Air force again in 1944. He recalls: "You know - fill out a form that asks, "Have you previously applied to join the Air Force? - No - OK you'll hear from us." and then "We refer to our previous letter, our decision cannot be altered." That reply was received on the 25 August 1944. "So I thought that's the army and that's the Air force and I'm not going to join the navy because I can't swim."

1942 saw the American military presence in Brisbane and the war occupying the thoughts of most adults of the city, not to mention Australia. There was great political tension between Australia and England as Prime Ministers Churchill and Curtin fought over the priorities of war. As Pee Wee was marching around Syria in February 1942, keeping the Germans at bay, Curtin was ordering a change in direction for a convoy of Australian troops. The 6th and 7th AIF Divisions were on board ships headed from the Middle East for Rangoon in Burma to stop the Japanese advance. Churchill and Roosevelt both felt this necessary, however Curtin and the Australian military Chiefs were able to prevail and have the troops sent home for the defense of Australia.

Many Australians were in fear of what the Japanese might do if they invaded. In 1942, after the fall of Singapore in mid February, the idea of the British defending Australia had been exposed as a strategic myth. Lee Kuan Yew, who later became the first Prime Minister of Singapore, was twenty years old at the time. He vividly recalls the Japanese invasion:

"The superior status of the British in Government and society was simply a fact of life. They had the biggest Empire history had ever known. ….I was brought up by my parents and grandparents to accept that this was the natural order of things…This was the Malaya and Singapore that 60,000 attacking Japanese soldiers captured, together with more than 130,000 British, Indian and Australian troops. In 70 days of surprises, upsets and stupidities, British Colonial society was shattered, and with it all the assumptions of the Englishman's superiority. The Asiatics were the ones who were supposed to panic. It was the white civilians who left the hospitals and public utilities unattended and fled to Singapore."[4]

Newspaper headlines screamed alarm in Australia and Britain. Churchill is know to have remarked in his memoirs that Singapore was the "Greatest capitulation in British Military history." However there were many factors that led to its fall. The Japanese employed superior tactics, weapons, aircraft and intelligence, while lack of training and preparation, by the allies, contributed to the defeat. There was fierce fighting and the Australian 22nd Brigade fought heroically with the 2/18th division losing half it's men before being overrun. Lee goes on to recount the horrors of the Japanese occupation, the torture and mass murder of civilians. If they could overrun the biggest British outpost in Asia so easily, "What might they do in Australia?", was the question on everyone's mind.

Japanese atrocities in China were well documented and Australian civilians had every reason to be apprehensive. From the Pearl Harbor attack on the 7th December 1941 to the fall of Singapore on the 15th February 1942 and then the bombing of Darwin on the 19th February, just four days later, the Japanese had taken total command of the Northern approaches to Australia, and might attempt a landing at any time. The suddenness and rapidity of these events shocked the nation. The Japanese had real momentum and something drastic needed to be done if they were to be stopped.

Poster published 1942. AWM 09225

There has been much debate as to whether they intended to or had the resources to invade Australia. Some say they knew they lacked the capacity to do so, others point to planning that had been done and maps drawn up for the control of northern Australia. There is evidence for both arguments. These matters are dealt with in exhaustive detail by Peter Stanley in his excellent 2006 work, "Invading Australia."

This book does not attempt to answer the question, instead it is personal responses to the threat, the fears and attitude of the people that are most interesting. The dramatic events of 1941 and 42 had a profound impact Australia. A large percentage of the population was convinced the Japanese were intent on invading. Newspaper stories were often illustrated with maps showing the Japanese advance down the Malaya peninsular, with lots of big red arrows pointing south.

One digger remarked:
"I joined up on New Year's day 1942. At this time the Jap was coming down the Malay Peninsula and an invasion of Australia was feared. Houses in Cairns, good houses were going for 40 pounds. Everyone was heading south." George Wilcox 39th battalion.[5]

The Royal Australian Air Force had no capacity to prevent the Japanese Air force from reaching Brisbane and although not widely known at the time, Townsville was bombed several times in July 1942. In fact it was a mad rush and in some cases panic for the Government and the population to gear up for the battles that were literally just over the horizon. The Battle of the Coral Sea, fought early May 1942 and then The Battle of Midway in the first week of June that year were titanic clashes between the United States and Japanese navies. The first was inconclusive but it's effect was to halt the Japanese naval advance in the South West Pacific. The Midway battle was a clear victory to the US forces which caught a large number of Japanese planes refueling on the decks of their ships. Three aircraft carriers were sunk and this turned the Pacific naval war in America's favor. Whatever possibility of invasion existed, it disappeared after this battle. However it was some time before this was generally realized.

As the navies confronted each other in the seas east of Townsville and further north at Midway island, Brisbane was flooded with American serviceman, heightening the sense of drama. Men and equipment poured forth from the ships docked at the wharf. The people of Brisbane were in awe of the scale and power of the American deployment. This was to be the invasion Brisbane experienced. The 2/15th battalion in Syria at the time, was thinking of home and Jim was writing his letter about wanting to come back and fight the Japanese.

"I am still living in hope of getting back before the Japs try to make a landing there although I don't think they could do it. Well Keith have you finished your air raid shelter yet, I don't think you will be needing it, I hope so anyhow." Jim Sedawie, Syria, 1942

Dad was fond of telling how, "Early in the piece I dug a big hole in the back yard and put sand bags around it, the neighbors thought I was a fool and laughed at me. When they bombed Darwin they stopped laughing and built their own shelters."

Allied calculations of whether the Japanese would attempt an invasion or not were uncertain at best. It seems that the most the Japanese were planning or were capable of was possibly occupying Darwin as a way of cutting the Allies movements and supply lines for the Western Pacific theatre. Control of the sea lanes from the Indian Ocean past Singapore and into the Western Pacific was in Japanese hands. However, it is clear is that most Australians prepared as though an invasion was likely. Brisbane was never bombed but that did not stop the citizens preparing as though they were about to be and most people had an air raid shelter or access to one. The proximity of the war felt most keenly when the Australian hospital ship, was sunk by a Japanese submarine in near North Stradbroke Island, east of Brisbane. The boat had large red crosses on a white background.

Two Hundred and sixth eight passengers, crew and medical personnel were killed. Brisbane people were shocked and the sinking was regarded as a war crime. Although this occurred in 1943, after the threat of invasion had passed, Brisbane people would have been very angry and distressed. The wreak was found in 2009.

Allison Flaherty, nee Harding, my mother in law, lived in Holland St. Toowong during the war; she was 11 years old at the time peace was declared, these are her recollections:

"My farther Alec Harding worked for the Post Master General and was not allowed to go to war. He knew Morse code and worked for the army. He did not talk about his work. On weekends he would teach others Morse code. He and a neighbor Col Lewis dug a bomb shelter in the back yard of Mrs. Dewintin's house, she was a widow. He also went with other men to the Toowong Primary school and dug trenches for the school children. They were not very deep and were open. We were all given a wooden peg to bite on when the bombs dropped. I remember there being sense of anxiety, but things were not talked about in front of the children. Food was rationed, a neighbor would give us a couple of eggs and they seemed like the crown jewels. Butter was rare and a lady next door used to make cookies out of dripping but I wouldn't eat them they were awful. Our mother used to take us on picnics into the Botanical Gardens in the city and one day the air raid siren went and we went into the bomb shelter, it was made of thick concrete. Later the all clear sounded. We heard that it had been a Japanese reconnaissance plane. In my year 7 at school I was sent to live with my Uncle in Stanthorpe for a year at a one-teacher school. On the day peace was declared our mother took us into town, there were hundreds of people and some were throwing coins in the air. My sister picked up two shillings which would be like $40 today. It was a great relief."[6]

Around the river, protecting the wharfs and ships, were anti aircraft batteries on the point at Newstead Park and Breakfast Creek, where the American Australian Memorial stands today. Brisbane was prickling with anti aircraft guns. The priority of air defenses were the ships, the port facilities, the major airports and then the city. Fixed gun batteries of 3.7inch anti-aircraft guns were located along the Brisbane River at Lytton, Balmoral, on the hill above cemetery, Hemmant, Pinkenba, Hendra, and Victoria Park. Keith used to man a 3.7 during his time off while working at the airport.[7]

Most of the major buildings in the city had sand bag blast walls built around them and there were many air raid shelters. Slit trenches and shelters were constructed at most schools and kids joined in, usually seeing the whole affair as a bit of fun. However the Brisbane City Council took the possibility of air raids and invasion very seriously as its annual report of 1941-42 records:

"Street lighting was disconnected or shaded and air raid warning sirens installed. The City Council built over 260 public air raid shelters and around 10,000 feet of slit trenches. Air raid wardens maintained blackout regulations throughout Brisbane."[8]

It was also recorded that many local councils who were expected to fund the construction of shelters, needed financial assistance from the state Government to carry out the work. In February 1942 the Queensland Government commissioned the building of extensive air raid shelters in the Botanic Gardens in Brisbane. Being the seat of Government this district was where most executive functions of government were carried out. Each of several shelters were to house 50 people and were sunk 5 feet below ground while extending 2 feet above.[9]

Darwin was bombed over sixty times and Townsville three times with numerous minor raids at islands and outposts in the north.[10]

There are still lots of relics scattered around Brisbane and other parts of Queensland for that matter and heritage groups are able to locate their whereabouts. On a recent trip to Maryborough I was interested to see a well preserved shelter in the grounds of the main railway station.

However it came to pass the bombs never fell on Brisbane and towards the end of 1942, the threat had passed. Gradually the people of Brisbane could relax back into a more ordered life and concentrate on the war effort. The shelter in the back yard in Toowong filled with water and it was a long time before it was taken down.

The dramatic events of the last year had had a deep impression. Most of Australia's thoughts were now preoccupied by conflict with the Japanese and the Allied successes at the battle of the Coral Sea and Midway. Not as many were aware of what was happening with the 9th Div and the struggle for ascendency in the Middle East, as opposing armies sought to gain an advantage.

CHAPTER FIVE

THE ENDLESS PATROL, PALESTINE & SYRIA

After Tobruk, the battalion was transported from Alexandria to Hill 69 which was near Gaza. Arriving in Palestine they made camp and from late October to December 1941 the battalion spent time reorganizing and training. New equipment was delivered and the bravery awards won in Tobruk were given to various members.

Post card Fragment with Jim, O'Neill Collection

They formed a regimental band and held concerts and plays which did much to keep spirits up. Leave came later and many had the opportunity to visit famous landmarks, some being in the footsteps of the first AIF who were in Egypt during the First World War. Jim's photo collection from this time includes Cairo, Alexandria, Tel Aviv & Tiberius. They stopped at Jaffa in Palestine where they practiced at a shooting range, and passed through Gaza. They were heading for Syria and a stint of garrison duty.

Syria had been the theatre for some confusing and contradictory actions regarding the French Vichy regime, the Germans and the Free French. In June 1942 the Australian 7th division along with Free French, British and Indian troops, invaded Syria and Lebanon. The allies apparently had word that the Vichy French Government of Syria had decided to invite Germany to station troops there. This was perceived as enough of a threat to warrant military action. In a short and bloody campaign the Vichy French were defeated and the Allies took control of this section of territory with the intention of protecting their flank against German movements through Turkey. So it fell to the 2/15th to guard the frontier from invasion. This was going to require covering of a lot of ground and so the boys had to go marching all over Northern Syria.

Although the battalion's time in Syria was to be a peaceful one, some might say a holiday, after Tobruk, it was not going to be easy, as their Commanding officers devised some punishing training and patrols, including what was dubbed "The Long March". Devised by Colonel Ogel, it was from Idlib to Lattika a distance of about 100kms, it purpose was to "toughen up the men."

As if the men needed "toughening up" after eight months in Tobruk.

Jim's letter from Syria 17th April 1942 is after three months of hard training and marching.

"I have been very busy lately I have marched all over Syria nearly, our last trip was 100 miles, arrived last night, today to spell, we will be off again early in the morning, we have a lot of country to guard, and we are expecting the Germans to try and break through any tick of the clock. I am terribly tired as our last day's marching was twenty four and a half miles, some marching eh?"

Roman Ruins Photo. J.Sedawie, O'Neill Collection

It seems the Officers and higher up's kept the boys on their toes with the threat of imminent invasion. Whether this was true or not is a moot point. They were in Syria from January to the end of June 1942, however the Germans did not invade as they were too busy fighting the Russians. On guard duty in the north near Aleepo two men were killed by a truck and due to the severe conditions Private Laurie died and was buried in the French cemetery.

It was freezing cold and there was heavy snow all about. A 9th Division skiing section was assembled and was said to have had a great time but very strenuous. Jim took lots of photos in of the snow in Syria and of Long John Cunningham, his officer, of whom he was very fond, referring to him in his letter,

"I have enclosed a snap also of myself and my officer Lt. Cunningham, Truth would only be too please to print it as he is the youngest son of the late Mr. A.H.W. Cunningham who owned Strathmore and other stations he died in February, he was the biggest racehorse owner in Australia, he comes from Nth Queensland, the truth gave him a great write up, and this is the first photo he will have of his son who served in Tobruk and is now in Syria. Or else you can give them the one in the snow with A.I.F 1942 2/15 on it." April 1942.

Photos J.Sedawie, O'Neill Collection

Jim and Long John were great mates and shared many lighter moments. There were lots of snow fights, time off in various towns and a chance to meet new people and talk to strangers. Having a hot bath was an uncommon luxury for the soldiers, especially after their earlier deprivations. Sharing coffee with the locals and visiting many ancient ruins, was pretty exciting and some fun was had riding donkeys. They often had trouble with the "Wogs" as the locals were known. Casual workers and hangers on would be up to mischief, trying to steal rifles and all manner of things. Quite a cultural experience, for a mob of blokes from Queensland! Not since the diggers of the First World War had so many Aussies been to the Middle East. In such lonely and isolated country it is clear that the men were homesick and sorely missed female company and familiar surroundings. More than once Jim mentions, Keith's mother and girls back home and his anxiety about being stranded in the war.

> Dear Keith,
> "Your ever welcome letter to hand last night and don't you know how pleased I was to hear from you, but I never received a letter from your mother, it is months since I had one from her."
>
> Well Keith I told you in my last letter that I made a new ring just like your mother's and Glady's ring with a heart.... Well Keith how are things at home are you still working, does Glady like married life. I suppose you will be the next to go off, do you still write to that girl from Toowoomba, that was a nice snap of her you sent me…………..I am only hoping to Christ that they send us home, that will be the day of all days, every time we reach the coast and see the sea, the first thing we do is look for a convoy, hoping that they are going to send us secretly away."
> Syria April 1942

This was from a bloke who had been through "some deadly battles" and had lived a harsh and unforgiving life for more than a year, seen friend's die in battle and witnessed the terrifying events of blitzkrieg. Yet he still express a deep tenderness and longing for normal life with the company of the ones he loved. Such is the contradictions of the life of the soldier. The family must have been relived that Jim was out of Tobruk and not in harm's way. Back home Keith was building ships and digging air raid shelters in the back yard. Brisbane was working it's way into a state of near panic as the threat of invasion loomed over the horizon and the whole country geared up for war with the Japanese.

"The Long March", as it was called was an exercise in patrolling but also a way of keeping the men fit and battle hardened as they knew they would be going back to the front in the not too distant future. Colonel Ogel had the idea to march the men from Idlid to Lattakia about 75miles as part of the "toughening up "process." (Austin 114)

Jim seemed pretty unimpressed with this idea, he would have preferred to be facing the Japanese. The 27th April 1942, was just after the fall of Singapore and before the Coral Sea battle, when their advances were at their peak. He writes,

"Well Keith I suppose you are under the same impression as a lot of people in Aussie that the 9th Division volunteered to stay over here, I believe Mr. Curtin said so, well he is a bloody liar, but I am still living in hopes of getting back before the Japs try to make a landing there although I don't think they could do it."

Jack Anning was in Syria with Jim, his feeling was "They (the Japanese) were very very close. We used to have "indignation meetings" where we would get around a talk about going home to fight the Japs. All ranks were upset that Australia was in danger and we could not go home. I thought about this, you see, my family and property where I was from in North Queensland, outside Charters Towers, would have been one of the areas they would have exploited for food and supplies if they had got in. I often thought that if I had of known that the Japanese would join the war and Australia would be threatened then I would never have volunteered to go overseas. All the boys from North Queensland were very keen to get back.

It was no surprise the whole of the battalion was anxious to be back. Not that they had a choice, as Gordon explains,

"We were in the 30th Brigade of the British Army and they didn't want us to go back, we had no say in the matter. Montgomery wanted the 9th Div to stay and he said later that, he would have been very pleased to have them for the invasion of Europe. Some of the blokes were sent white feathers from Australia, accusing the men of being cowards for not wanting to go back and defend Australia. These were probably relatives of some of the poor buggers."

Jack received one of these feathers and recalls it must have come from someone in Townsville. He also received a "Dear John" letter as he called. His girlfriend back home bidding him goodbye for another man. However Jack was not bitter and remarked to me that in some ways he was glad he had been to North Africa, as it had made him a experienced soldier, much better prepared for the challenges of the New Guinea campaign. The jungle didn't worry him, "to me it was just like a lot of overgrown bush" he said.

Curtin argued with Churchill and Roosevelt about the return of Australian troops and eventually prevailed. Frustration built within the 9th Div, as the Australian 6th and 7th divisions had been withdrawn to Australia and the Japanese forces had extended their reach to New Guinea, but the 9th Div had to wait till January 1943 before eventually going home, however this was not before they were to see action again in North Africa.

While the Battalion was in Syria, British and German forces in North Africa pounded each other, covering vast areas with move and counter move. The Germans gained a significant advantage when they took Crete, after kicking the Allies out of Greece. The situation became desperate for the British, and they brought forward "Operation Battle Axe" with the intention of retaking much lost ground and retaking Tobruk. Churchill was adamant that one big push could dislodge Rommel and put pressure on his generals, Alexander and Auchinleck to make the decisive push. This ended in disaster with the rout at "Hell Fire Pass" putting the British position in Egypt under severe pressure. Auchinleck, removed from command was replaced by General Montgomery, who eventually was to get the equipment he needed.

Gordon recalls that at this stage it was a battle of logistics as each army tried desperately to gain an armoured advantage. The sea transports were harassed and at times sunk, the British losing fifty tanks in one ship.

On the 21st of June news came through of the fall of Tobruk, the Battalion history records that the men were depressed at the news. Rommel was not the type to give up easily and now that Tobruk had fallen the allied position in North Africa was deteriorating quickly. The 9th Div, was rushed in to hold the northern sector along the coast of Egypt. The war in the desert was heading towards its inevitable climax and Jim was heading into his most dangerous and risky part of the conflict. They were not told where they were they were headed, they had to work it out themselves. Leaving Syria, on a train the realization hit that they were not going down the Suez Canal to Australia, but were heading west. They were going back to North Africa.

Jack recalls,
"The Brits were losing ground against Rommel and the Australians and New Zealanders were called in to hold them back until they could build up enough strength. We were told by Montgomery,

"Win this and you can go home. This was told to us as an added incentive."

Montgomery had often referred to the 9th Div as his "secret weapon". He had pushed hard to keep them in the Middle East, knowing what they were capable of. Morale and motivation are key factors in how soldiers commit themselves to battle and it was in this frame of mind that the Australians went to back to North Africa, not happy that Tobruk had been lost after all their effort and cranky that they were not going back to Australia.

"Win this and you can go home."

CHAPTER SIX

EL ALAMEIN AND THE BATTLE FOR PEE WEE RIDGE

The period between the withdrawal of the Division from Tobruk and the beginning of the first battle of El Alamein, was filled with thrust and counter thrust between the opposing armies. The War in the Desert had so far been inconclusive. While Rommel was the undisputed master of his forces Churchill was ever critical of his commanders. In the first week of July 1942, General Archibald Wavell was replaced by the "Auch" and he was given express orders to launch a counter-attack. The next phase of the campaign saw the two armies exchange blows across vast expanses of desert. The British suffered some severe setbacks including operations Brevity and Battle Axe. The latter was intended to relieve the siege of Tobruk but ended in disaster with the loss 220 tanks, while the Germans lost less than 20. With the Allied signals Rommel obtained from a compromised American code, he had a huge advantage and had positioned his forces opposing the British along what was known as the Gazala line. He inflicted a heavy defeat on Auchinlek's forces and captured Tobruk in one day securing vast amounts of supplies and a sea port. Hitler rewarded him by making him the youngest ever field marshal, yet he was known to remark that another Panzer regiment would have been better.

The British had to retreat back into Egypt and Auchinlek withdrew his forces to El Alamein, the best defensive position but only about one hundred kilometres from Alexandria. Churchill was furious that he had put so much effort, men and equipment into the campaign and still the British were not certain about holding the Suez and Egypt. El Alamein is in unforgiving desert country, 260 km north west of Cairo which is today, 3 hours 38 minutes driving time. It only takes a glance at a map to see why Tobruk was considered vital and how much was at stake. Rommel and the Africa Corps were now close to the main cities of Egypt and the Suez canal. If their advance had made it to either Alexandria or Cairo the ensuing chaos would have been impossible to contain. Churchill replaced Auchinlek with General Bernard Montgomery, a controversial figure but one known for being hard headed and with a determination to win battles.

The Allies prepared themselves for the massive battle they knew was ahead. The 9th Division and 2/15th was moved by truck and train to Amriya, before moving to the El Alamein area on 06 July. With enemy gun flashes on the horizon, they moved closer and dug in on the 09 July.

The chain of command was such that General Alexander was Montgomery's superior. However it was the latter who would take operational command of the Eight Army. Montgomery had been given a mandate to destroy the Axis forces in North Africa. Any further withdrawal was out of the question. Knowing that Rommel's successes were based on his superior mobile tactics, he decided on a more static strategy. Massive defensive lines, consisting of hundreds of thousands of mines were built by both armies. Montgomery waited. He would not be happy if Rommel attacked too soon but after he was ready, he would welcome it. Having resisted the pressure from Churchill and others to attack quickly, he assembled a force of 220,000 men, 1100 tanks and 900 field guns. This was twice the number of tanks and guns of the Africa Corps. He positioned his forces between the coast and the Quttra depression, a vast impassable sand desert. This closed down the space, preventing Rommel from using is usual flanking tactics. It was to be a head on confrontation.

Many histories have been written about "Monty" - how he was a great General, how he made a mess at operation "Market Garden" in Normandy, how he was arrogant and overbearing and had gotten all the Americans off side - yet something of his character is revealed by his interactions with the Australians. He arrived at the forward post of the 20th Brigade and called for an Australian Army slouch hat, which he promptly wore. The story goes that it looked a bit awkward but his gesture of solidarity was not lost on the men.

Montgomery then asked for and was given a "Rising Sun" badge for the hat, claiming an entitlement to wear it on the ground that his father had been Bishop of Tasmania. As a leader his methods were to visit the front line, inspect no man's land and be visible to his men. He felt that morale was the most important aspect of an army's preparation and that this had to be maintained through a show of resolve and confidence in the men. After he had taken command, he restructured the formations of the army and changed the way the army would fight. Morale was immediately strengthened. Upon visiting the 2/15th battalion he said,

"This is good ground, when the enemy attacks, as he will, you will stay here. If you are surrounded you stay surrounded. You have fought for this ground and you have won it, and you will not give it up.... I repeat you will stay here. Good morning." Colonel Grace remarked "You could feel the change, after all the withdrawals from the western parts of the field. From that day on there was never any talk of going back."[1]

The General felt his army was ready to confront the Africa Corps. However one aspect of his and the British leadership that rankled the Australians was the fact that English officers were put in positions of command often above more experienced Australians. The official records devote some several pages to the machinations regarding the various appointments of middle level commanders. One in particular was the case of General Morshead, the hero of Tobruk being passed over because he had not had the requisite training and experience and had not been a soldier all his life. This was humiliating for Morshead to have "Pommy" General staff flown out from England to be in command over him. The incident was the subject of a number of cables being between Churchill, Curtin and Blamey. The English attitude to "Dominion" staff was typically of superiority, even though Morshead, a hero of Tobruk had proved his worth.

The build up for El Alamein continued apace as the Axis and allied armies relied on their sea borne supplies to give them an advantage. Much shipping was lost by both sides as they ran the gauntlet of dive bombers, u-boats, destroyers, and cruisers, not to mention anti aircraft fire, sea mines, sabotage and bad weather. The industrial production of the competing nations struggled to gain an advantage. The Americans having agreed to a "Germany first policy" in support of the British, were getting closer to a full war production. The German military industrial complex had been at full production for some years but supplies to Rommel had to compete with the now massive undertaking of invading Russia.

Both sides manoeuvred for position while the Australians continued their practice of aggressive patrolling. Gordon recalls the "men were fighting and being killed all the time, not just in the big battles." The following incident he recalls from the time of El Alamein:

"One evening on the line just on dusk I heard a noise he thought was a tank but it turned out to be a truck. It was quite dark and I was nearly going to call out "Hey Butch what the bloody hell are you doing out there?" Butch was the quartermaster and I thought he might have been lost bringing rations up. Any way they were about thirty yards away and I heard them talking in German. I got a rifle and fired at them and then asked for a Thompson, I was firing and I called out to Alec Else - "Alec quick Jerry" and we got stuck into them with the Bren. I had shot one of them and I went out to get his papers, see who they were. He was yelling and kicking his guts out. Anyhow Blinko called out to me, "Put the poor bastard out of his misery" I didn't have the guts to, I reckoned if they were standing up it was ok but when he was down as far as I was concerned it was murder. Anyway as I lay out there with him this thing stared to explode and was blowing up over our heads. Next morning the only thing left was the corner of the cab of the truck. I came back with the best pair of field glasses I had ever seen. Anyhow the day after that, these two blokes, a tall thin bloke and a short nuggety bloke were walking towards headquarters. It was the Brigadier and I thought the nuggety bloke was his batman. This bloke came over to our position and starting talking to us. Just in shorts and a tin hat. Incidentally this truck with just the corner post left on it, the Jerries ranged on to it and were shelling Christ out of us. Every twenty minutes we were copping it.

Any way Blinko says to this bloke, "Hey mate you better hop in this trench as we're getting shelled pretty regularly." He hopped in and we got shelled when he was there. We talked of everything and anything except the army and what was going on. Later he said "Well I better go and get the Brigadier." He never had any badges or rank on, he hopped out of the pit, never said a word, took his tin hat off and put a soft top cap on with red braid around it and said "Well I'll see you blokes later." And away he went. I said to Blinko, "Do you know who that is, He said No. I said that's Morshead. "Ah Bullshit" he said "generals don't come out here." "Well that one did I said." He didn't let on who he was, but just by putting on his cap he let us know. That's the type of bloke he was. He was solid, they used to call him Ming the Merciless, he would never cop no bloody rubbish, he expected us to do a job. But how many Generals would do that?" Gordon 2012.

The Australian trenches were often within mortar range, being shelled on a regular basis. In order to combat this, patrols were sent out. On 04 August the Battalion was visited by General Morshead and Brigadier Windeyer. That night A coy. of the 2/15th were led on patrol by Captain Bill Cobb. The orders to the "fighting patrol" were to capture enemy prisoners and obtain identification. Two NCO's and 10 soldiers left their position at 9 pm and travelled about 1500 yards towards the enemy positions. They bumped into a couple of enemy sentry positions and were challenged. Realising that the element of surprise was lost, the patrol instantly threw grenades and charged. They inflicted several causalities and received two themselves, with one dead. They also captured an enemy soldier but in the process of bringing him back to their lines they ran into trouble. A German with a Spandau machine gun opened fire from a trench and killed the prisoner while at the same time wounding Captain Cobb in the arm. He subsequently blacked out on the way back to their lines whereupon Corporal Else carried him until they found an Italian stretcher bearer. He later regained consciousness and was OK."

Was Pee Wee In this patrol? We cannot be certain. However he was on active duty at the time and he'd had plenty of practice in Tobruk, he was a wily and experienced soldier.

"Pee Wee" Sedawie was a "scrounger" as Keith would say. A bit of a bower bird, he would collect stuff as a lot of other soldiers would. His letters often mention some of the things he collected and was sending back to Australia. In one letter he says:

"I am going to send you a couple of souvenirs and a couple of helmets. I will also send you two big shells which you can make into pint pots, the officer came round the other day and took all the field glasses and revolvers off the boys, but I still have your rifle."

And he later says:

"I have sent you about a dozen parcels, all war souvenirs I also sent you the rifle and ammunition but I forgot to tell you that I got 4 hacksaw blades and about seven files from a German tank which we blew up. ... I sent you egg cups, German crash helmets, dust glasses, pint pots, a big knife and 2 leather coats. I have a watch I am going to send you, it was going when I took it off the Hun, but it has since stopped. I have German bayonet and I have a belt with all different types of badges I will also send you. I am also post the last of the souvenirs for you from Tobruk you will get them before Christmas".[2]

Remarkably when talking with Jack about Pee Wee and this letter, he mentioned that he had a ring that was made by a bloke in the Battalion. It was made from a piece of propeller that came from the Italian plane that he shot down while in Tobruk. It had two pieces of a toothbrush cut and fitted into the ring in the Battalion colours. Astounded I told him "I have got that piece of propeller on my book case. My Old Man gave it to me years ago." He remarked that he wore his ring until in New Guinea he got sick, lost weight and it fell off his hand. Fishing out the piece of propeller from the book case I was happy to know it was still there. Pee Wee's letter from Syria says,

"Well Keith, I told you in my last letter that I made a new ring just like your mother's and Gladys' ring with a heart, well one of the engineers is putting my colours in it."

Collecting and making things was a way of passing the time. Pee Wee was a curious type as he was always on the look out to add to his collection. This trait would be his undoing. On the morning of 07 August his curiosity got the better of him and a couple of mates. They went out in to no-mans-land on a scrounging expedition under the cover of fog. The field in front of the lines was often strewn with stuff left behind, sometimes in a hurry and often useful equipment was to be found. They had spotted a derelict truck in no-mans-land and were determined to have a look.

What happened next comes from the battalion history, as told by Phil O'Brien and Cliff Duel, and from the July 2012 interview with Jack Anning. Phil says

"Out in front of A Company was a knocked out English supply truck and it looked along way out so one morning no-mans-land when the fog was very thick, Carl Huddy, Bob White and Pee Wee Sedawie decided to go out and examine the truck and see if it contained anything worthwhile, but the fog bamboozled them as fogs do in the Western Desert. They lift suddenly, just like a raising curtain and that's just what the fog did and our friends suddenly found themselves virtually among a number of German soldiers, having their breakfast, and the reaction was instant on both sides. At the same time Cliff and his mate Jack Collyer had debated the merits of going out with Cliff insisting that they tell "Long John" Cunningham their officer.

I said "don't tell him he won't let us go out" but Jack told him he wouldn't let them go out saying the fog would lift. However the two went anyway.

"After about half an hour we hadn't found anything, but the fog started to lift just as Long John had said, it lifted very fast. Suddenly a Spandau opened up and we hit the dirt very fast. I looked around and to our left were two men running like hell for our wire, Jacko Huddy and Hambone Gilmore. We couldn't stop laughing as we thought we were the only ones out there. However the machine guns weren't firing at them either as there were no bullets around them. So we looked round and there down in front of us was Bob White and Jim (Pee Wee) Sedawie running like hell. Jack and I yelled to them to turn and come back to where we were but they suddenly disappeared down a hole."

"When we got back we went straight to Cunningham and told him what had happened. He sure told us off as expected, but then Bob White came in through the wire. He had made a run for it and was shot through the legs, but he was lucky as they were only flesh wounds."

"Earlier Pee Wee had called out "Get the artillery to fire and get me out."

Pee Wee & Long John. Photo Slouch Hat Publications

Cunningham then brought up a section with all the Bren guns and laid down a barrage. Long John had a voice like a fog horn. He called out to Pee Wee to make a run for it when we started firing. He didn't come out of the hole. Cunningham sent back for 3 inch mortars and laid down a barrage but to no avail. At that point Bob Ogle rang company HQ while this was going on and asked how the battle for "Pee Wee Ridge" was going. Eventually an artillery barrage was laid down".[3]

Jack Anning recalls:
"There was fire going both ways and it was pretty hot. The Germans were about 1000 yards away and Pee Wee was about 800 yards away. While the shooting was going on the men were organising a unit to go out and get him. This was taking a bit of time and had to be authorised

by the higher ups whether it was worth the risk or not. All this time they were closing in on him. We were close to being ready when we saw him being walked away under guard and then taken away in a small German vehicle, like a scout car. That was the last we saw of him."[4]

In fact Jack asked me if Pee Wee survived the war, as he had not seen him since coming home. When he saw his mate Bob White run for it and be shot through the legs, Pee Wee must have known that German guns were trained on his position. Not knowing Bob was only lightly wounded, he might have thought it could have been mortal. In late 2012 I made contact with Noel Sedawie, one of Pee Wee's nephews and it became clear why he didn't escape. He had been shot twice, once in the chest and once in the foot. Keith had told me about him having a bullet fragment in his lung but I had never put the two facts together. We can now understand why he did not make a run for it. At the battalion dinner in Brisbane on Anzac day 2009, Gordon said to me: "Pee Wee wasn't a coward he just didn't want to get killed."

Gordon didn't know he was wounded at the time.

Jack recalls Pee Wee "a good soldier but a bit too adventurous and it was sad, as he was a character and a number one scrounger."

He had some chance of getting out but there was also the possibility of being shot in the back. With two bullet wounds he was in not state to make a run for it. However as Gordon reckons he would have been treated well by the front line German troops, who respected the opposition troops, as "We lived the same life."

Pee Wee's service record states:
17.8.42 Battle casualty, reported missing in action, believed POW and added to "X" list.

This was the last anyone saw or heard of Pee Wee until the 02 June 1943 where his record states that he is now officially a POW. His letters would have stopped and the family back home would have been going through what many others were too. Not knowing what had happened to their loved ones.

The Africa Korps and Rommel were well known for their fair treatment towards prisoners. In fact Rommel was known to have torn up the "Commando Order" issued by Hitler to his Generals in secret on 18 October 1942. It required all enemy soldiers captured behind the lines to be executed immediately. Although contravening sections of the Geneva Convention, most of Hitler's Generals carried it out. Rommel was one of the few with the courage to deify Hitler. So Jim Sedawie was to become a beneficiary of Rommel's honour. It was when he got back to the rear positions where desk soldiers and other ranks were in charge that he would have been dealt with more harshly. A prisoner at such a critical time just before a major battle might have important information. Pee Wee would have been taken to a doctor but also would have been interrogated.

The historic struggle that culminated in the battle of El Alamein was only days away. The men of the 2/15th were desperate to avoid losing a man prisoner to the enemy and maintenance of secrecy was crucial. This was the motive behind the frantic efforts to get him out. One thing in his favour was that the Africa Corps was not run by the Gestapo, and there was no SS attachment. One can only assume this was at Rommel's insistence. The Africa Corps had shown their character by the way they had treated prisoners, allowing the Allies to collect their dead and by observing informal truces.

It has been said the Western desert campaign was a "War without hate". Two groups of professional soldiers who learnt grudging respect for each other, who gave no quarter when in battle but were able to retain some dignity. The fighting took place where there were no civilian casualties and little damage to cultural buildings and infrastructure. Exposed in the open desert it was man and machine against the other man and machine. Both sides were equally battered by wind, dust, heat, cold and thirst. Pee Wee had been through all this and although he was captured, he was not in danger, for him the fighting was over, but not for the Battalion.

The 2/15th was soon ordered into one of the most horrific episodes of their war. "Operation Bulimba", was to be a practice exercise for the Eight army as a whole. Montgomery decided that he had to change the way the army would fight. Instead of fighting in "Jock Columns", small units of combined infantry and motorised support, they were to fight as divisions and brigades. The previous battles and skirmishes conducted by Wavell had been inconclusive and at times disastrous. Montgomery was determined to maximise his logistical superiority.

British high command wanted to see how the new tactics would work against the Germans. Operation Bulimba was conceived out of the necessity to reconfigure the Army's fighting units. The 2/15th relieved the 2/28th Infantry Battalion, holding the line from Hill 33 to the coast throughout August. On 01 September the 2/15th participated in Operation Bulimba. The planning for this "Stunt" as it was referred to, began as a raid, the plan was to get in and get out quickly. Without proper intent it evolved into a full battalion assault with the intention of holding enemy ground for nine hours.

And so minus Pee Wee, the 2/15th was sent into battle on 01 September. What resulted was vicious hand to hand fighting in exposed ground, mayhem and confusion. One excerpt from the Battalion history gives an impression of what it was like.

"Corporal Horton McLaughlin charged an enemy post that was holding up the advance of his section. McLaughlin having bayoneted three enemies in the post, then grabbed a sub machine gun from one of the wounded Germans and attacked the adjacent post, killing all four occupants. His next target was a post about 200 yards further on, which he attacked, killing four of the defenders with grenades. Having run out of ammunition McLaughlin then attacked the remaining four Germans, swinging his empty Tommy gun as a club. When one of the enemy attacked him, he knocked him out with a well aimed kick, then finished off the rest of the post with grenades. He was later awarded the DCM."[5]

Communication lines were broken, several officers killed and the fog of battle descended over the field. Acts of bravery were common as comrades ferried wounded back to the wire and came forward in the attack. The Germans were able to direct the fire of 100 artillery pieces onto the field as well as untold machine guns, mortars and mines. The battalion lost 8 of its 11 Bren gun carriers. And although their objectives were achieved they eventually were ordered to withdraw, which they did in an orderly fashion under the command of Major Colin Grace who had replaced Colonel Ogle, who was badly wounded. One hundred and forty enemy prisoners were taken and upwards of one hundred and fifty killed.

However the battalion lost 59 men who were killed or died of their wounds, 109 wounded and 25 missing. The wounded were ferried from the battle field by the Carrier Platoon, with Jack Anning in command of one. About half their fighting strength was lost, a terrible blow. All this in the space of two hours, and for what, was the question many asked at the time. And so, as fate would have it Pee Wee was absent from the worst fighting in the desert campaign. Our story would certainly be very different if he was not a prisoner at the time. "Brian Chase described Bulimba as being a tragic waste of the cream of the battalion."[6]

The operation generated distrust between the Australians and the British, especially as tanks would only move under British orders. And as Gordon remarked:

"They left us stranded. As soon as one was knocked out the rest retreated."

The Australians had to retreat under fire and did so in an orderly fashion, Gordon was lucky to survive as he lost many mates that day. Bulimba demonstrated that the Eight Army did not know how to co-ordinate tank and infantry attacks or how to manoeuvre in close quarters, something Rommel and the Africa Korps had mastered in their European campaigns of 1939 -40. It would seem that the ultimate objective of Bulimba was never decided upon and therefore its execution was a disaster. This inconclusive and costly battle showed Montgomery that his tactics were seriously wanting and this was achieved at great cost of Australian lives.

It was now obvious that Montgomery had serious problems to solve. But as events took their course, the balance of power was turning towards the British. Hitler and the German high command were preoccupied with the Russian front, and the terrible battle for Stalingrad. The Africa Korps was left critically short of fuel and other supplies. Gordon remarked "I could have won the Battle of El Alamein as Montgomery had waited till he had overwhelming fire power and resources before launching his final assault."

Montgomery stated before the start of the battle: "The battle which is about to begin will be one of the decisive battles of history. It will be the turning point of the war. Let every officer and man enter the battle with a stout heart and with the determination to do his duty so long as he has breath in his body. And let no man surrender as long as he is unwounded and can fight."[7]

Operation Supercharge began with an unholy artillery barrage, lasting for six hours and lighting up the whole horizon. The Eight Army advanced and punched through the German defences but was stopped by their fierce resistance. Monty resorted to his secret weapon - the Australian 9th Div. They were ordered to go in against the enemy lines near the coast road to create a diversion and draw in the opposing forces. Rommel who had always feared the Australians' ability, brought the full force of the Africa Korps to bear down upon the Aussies, thus creating an opening for the British to smash through Italian lines further south. This action proved to be one of the great turning points of the North Africa campaign and indeed the Second World War. Whatever the "Pommies" might have said about the "Colonials" they knew that their courage and ability was second to none. The 2/15th went into battle at El Alamein a depleted force, but continued to distinguish itself. More great men were lost before Rommel was vanquished and the battalion brought back to

Australia. Their last engagement was to chase down and capture the tail of the retreating Germans.

Arriving at Sydney they were given a rousing welcome by General Morshead and various military personnel and the Australian people. The Queenslanders soon boarded a train and arrived in Brisbane on 01 March 1943. They went on leave before going into Jungle training in preparation for the campaigns in New Guinea and Borneo. Meanwhile Pee Wee was holed up in an Italian POW camp in North Africa, enduring terrible conditions as he waited to be transferred to Italy.

In 2012 Gordon was chosen to be one of the Australian representatives to go with an official Australian contingent back to the battle field. Seventy years after surviving the horrors of war, the faces of his *cobbers* sprang up from their resting places as he walked among the lines of headstones. He is old now but his spirit is not dimmed, he cherishes his lost mates and keeps their memory alive.

CHAPTER SEVEN

POW

Pee Wee had gone into captivity on the 07 August 1942 and the battles of the North African campaign soon came to their inevitable climax. I'm not sure when Keith would have realised that something was wrong, but the news would have caught up with him while he was working at the airfield. I knew Pee Wee had been a POW and I have a map about the Empire in the war with his hand writing: "broadcast around Stalag xviii a the night of Feb 24,1945"

When I was first researching this story I stumbled across a copy of the official Battalion history, "Let Enemies Beware" in the Noosa library. Excited, I anxiously flicked it open. When I came to the pages with the story of how Pee Wee was captured and saw his photo with Long John Cunningham, I could hardly believe my eyes. I later showed this to Keith who was 86 at the time. He was a very surprised to say the least.

There is a lot of source material about POW's from WW 2 and many books have been written. I am indebted to those POW's and authors who have done the hard work of compiling the information that has given me such a great insight into Pee Wee's life. This story aims to give an accurate, but not exhaustive, account of what it was like for a POW (Pee Wee), what he went through and what he witnessed. Their life was at times very difficult to endure, at other times not as difficult. By the end of the war Pee Wee had been in captivity for three and a half years. His first few months must have been terrible, trying to recover from his wounds, on poor rations and suffering exposure. How he managed to survive at all is something of a mystery, but certainly it was an amazing feat of endurance. Some of the details are missing, however the history of the camps he was in and the route he took from capture in North Africa, to Italy, Germany the UK and finally Australia, is reasonably well documented.

He went into captivity knowing that his mates had tried to get him out and that he was facing interrogation and a long stint as a prisoner. When reading about POW's, a recurring theme is the shame they felt on being captured and their humiliation in being stripped of dignity and a feeling of helplessness. It must have been pretty distressing lying wounded in that hole in the ground with fire all around, mortars going off, knowing your mob was trying to get you out. The choice was to be either be killed or captured. Not a very nice place to be for a soldier. He was one of 1,941 soldiers of the 2/AIF captured in North Africa.

He would have been in a pretty bad state when captured, but the Germans would have taken him to a doctor. Their medical facilities were of a high standard and doctors well trained. They would have tended his wounds and made him reasonably comfortable.

After a short time he was handed over to the Italians, as the Germans had put them in charge of holding prisoners. This was because the Africa Corps was a fighting unit and most Germans were involved in front line duties. The Italians, not as committed to the battle, suffered from lack of leadership and training, so they were often relegated to support duties. As the Italian army began to realise the consequences of being Germany's ally and the impact the Allied war machine was having on their country, some resented the German influence in their lives. They had no particular hatred towards the British, but began to hate their own Government and Mussolini for what they had been led into.

Although the Italians "had no quarrel" with the British, this didn't translate into any special friendship with their prisoners who were captured in large numbers in North Africa, Greece and Crete. Initially they were in totally inadequate holding camps with no latrines, rotten food which was at time salvaged from blown up food dumps, no medical supplies or supervision and brutal guards. There were millions of flies, fleas and lice, making life unbearable. A putrid stench pervaded everything and there were no bathing facilities. Often men were captured in just the clothes they stood up in so they had no supplies or personal items.

Members of the 2/15th captured in the Benghazi Handicap were transported in open trucks to a camp at Sabratha. The conditions they endured were among the worst of the African camps. Mass dysentery occurred very soon after being captured and the men. Men queued to use the primitive latrines which they often failed to reach in time. With typical Australian laconic humour one wag was know to have commented that "He could bend over and hit a fly at twenty yards without the slightest effort, such was the pressure built up in his stomach system."[1]

Those captured later around El Alamein, at the time of the Battle of Bulimba, were held in a small enclosure at El Darba. Pee Wee would have been in this group. Ted Faulkes of the 2/32nd Infantry battalion AIF was captured in July 1942. From El Darba he was transported standing up in the back of an Italian truck, so crowded he was unable to sit down. The trip across the desert to a holding camp outside Benghazi, called "The Palms" was about 1000 kilometres away. Thirsty and hungry, the men were covered in lice. They were transferred to the main Benghazi camp after about four weeks where several thousand men of many different nationalities and in varying states of health lived. Malnutrition was common, conditions were appalling, the rations were terrible and many died.

Harry Pentecost, who was captured with some British troops near Derna and transferred to this transit camp, recalled:

"The local water was undrinkable unless boiled. I was one of the luckier ones as I was still mobile and did not have severe piles. Some were so bad they crawled to the latrine benches and never bothered to pull up their trousers, as it was a constant discharge of green excreta and the suffering of piles. I remember one man who went from fifteen stone to six stone in only a few weeks before he died."[2]

From this camp Jim would have been put on a boat for Italy. In some ways he was lucky to have made it as the Mediterranean was a dangerous place in those days. Despite the Red Cross trying to mediate a truce for the protection of POW vessels, this did not come about. A number were sunk. In August 1942 an Allied submarine torpedoed the Italian freighter *Nino Bixio*, killing more than 200 of the British and dominion prisoners aboard, including 37 of the 201 Australians."[3]

Ted Faulks recalled that after walking the five miles from Benghazi to the port, the group of about 500 men he was in were herded to the dock. The hold of the ship was awash with a fetid mixture of faces, urine and vomit. After a nightmare trip of three days without food they landed at Brindisi and were made to stagger through the streets as they were pelted with garbage and spat upon. Shortly after this he had his first proper wash in six months.[4]

Trooper Gilbert Knott who was in the 4th Royal Tank Regiment, 54th Royal Armored Corps served in Tobruk and was captured in June 1942 spending his initial period of captivity in another Italian camp before being transferred to Tuturano Campo 85. Pee Wee's record shows he was in P.G. 85 Tuturano on the Italian east coast near Brindisi. The POW system was overwhelmed by the number of prisoners, Trooper Gilbert records:
1942, 7 Wednesday –
Saw the MO. He told me I had lumbago and diarrhoea. He gave me some salts and told me not to eat anything.

13 Saturday –
A fellow named Maclean died today of malnutrition and dysentery. He makes the second one.

4 Friday - Learned that when this camp opened last August, 33 men died in 28 days. Recently one was shot trying to escape; Hayes of Liverpool. One has had his throat cut. Went to a concert given by Imps and Ragamuffins. Very good.[5]

I remember Dad telling me how Jim hated the Italian guards and it seems that the passage of time had not diminished his disdain. In Gurppignano, the Commandant and guards were renowned for their cruelty. They would often hit prisoners over the head with a rifle butt for no reason.

"On one occasion during a game of cricket an Australian, Edward Symonds, who had drunk some secret wine was cheering loudly. The guards taking offense, manhandled him and he resisted. His friends tried to calm him, but he was shot in the chest at close range and died in a few seconds. There was nothing his mates could do."[6]

Main gate PG 57 Gruppignano, North Italy, 1942. AWM p02793.001

Jim's service history records he was in campo 85 on the 30f June 1943, but this was almost a year after his capture, so he must have been in Italy for quite a while before this. Trooper Gilbert's diary begins in June 1942 probably a month or so before Jim arrived. The diary records that conditions improved as the Italians became better organised. At least it was a vast improvement on North Africa and with arrival of Red Cross packages which included cigarettes and better food, life would become more tolerable.

The conclusion of Montgomery's Operation Supercharge, drove the Germans out of North Africa and the 9th Division got a much needed rest. The last action the 2/15th saw in North Africa was to chase and capture some of the German rearguard in the first week of November 1942. On the 25th Of January 1943, they departed for Australia on the troop ship HMT Acquitania.

The Africa Corps retreated to Europe and with the Allies landing in Sicily on June 1943, the Italian Fascist government collapsed. Strangely, word was sent by British messengers to the Italian POW camps that prisoners should stay where they were, remain calm and they would be liberated. However out of about 80,000 that were in the camps, 52,000 were simply rounded up by the Germans and moved in haste to Germany.[7]

In Campo 57 Gruppignano where other members of the 2/15th were held, the Germans arrived in September 1943 and immediately loaded them on to a train for their journey to Stalag 18 A, Wolfsberg, a POW camp in Austria. The initial inmates of the war to arrive at Stalag 18A were 26,000 French soldiers who had been captured in the first engagements of the war where they were to spend nearly five years in captivity. It was said that they "Had the run of the place". These were the largest group, next were the Allies, including the Australians and New Zealanders whose numbers varied between 5000 and 11000. About 40 percent of these were Australians. There were also 10,000 Italians and 4000 Russians. Numbers varied over the course of the war but up to 48, 000 prisoners in total were housed at Stalag 18 A and surrounding work camps.[8]

There were British and Australian prisoners who had been captured in Crete in July 1941 after the Churchill inspired disaster that was the Allied defence of Greece. The Allied forces on Crete were overwhelmed by German paratroopers and sent to Wolfsberg. About 800 Australians were in the first lot to arrive. Although this was an area far removed from the front and was very picturesque with mountain villages and snow capped peaks, living conditions were very difficult to begin with. At first the men were billeted in a set of old stables with no furniture, one blanket and little clothing. With the onset of winter it became very cold, especially when the British officers refused to accept new issue of captured French uniforms. The men went without, three died of dysentery and there were several cases of malaria. After some months and by the time Jim would have arrived things began to improve.

"The atmosphere was totally different to Gruppignano. We were not plagued by petty Italian guards, we were freer to move about, black market trading with guards was more openly done and we were sent out of camp in work parties."[9]

In accordance with the terms of the Geneva Convention the camps were visited every three to four months by a person from the "Protecting Power" or the Red Cross, which produced excellent records of camp conditions. For the Allied troops the protecting power was initially the United States initially, it became Switzerland after the US had entered the war. Visiting officers were given free access to the prisoners and were allowed to interview in private the "Man of Confidence" for each camp who was an elected leader, usually a senior officer. He dealt with the leaders of the guards and organizational issues. Reports were sent back to the relevant authorities in the Switzerland, the UK and Australia and Red Cross copies were sent to the German authorities.

A feature of these reports was the variety in standards they applied to different camps at different times. After conditions improved initially, they declined significantly towards the end of the war. As Germany began to collapse, what was reported unsatisfactory at an early stage could be reported as satisfactory or even as good as things got grim towards the end. However, men were grateful to have shelter, food and protection from danger.

Jim arrived in Wolfsberg sometime between July and September 1943 when the summer weather would have been pleasant and conditions reasonable. After the Italians this must have been some relief. Rounded up by the advancing German army, the prisoners of Campo 85 were transported with typical efficiency to the waiting Stalag 18A. One of the more unsavoury aspects of the German industrial machine was the use of forced labour. As the war progressed and Germany became more desperate from lack of supplies and collapsing morale, conditions too became desperate. Coal mining was the most dangerous and sometimes deadly work. A few Aussies and many others were put through terrible slave-like regimes. However Jim was one of the lucky ones, relatively speaking, as the living and working conditions in his camp were usually humane and often not too onerous, although they were sometimes crowded and at times harsh.

German ideas of race and superiority were extended to all and there was a clear hierarchy of prisoners. French, English and Australians got the best treatment and were able to negotiate more civil conduct from their captors. Belgians, Dutch and Norwegians were a little below them. Then came the Serbs and Poles, stateless and with no protection and below them the Russians. These men were given the most inhumane and brutal treatment. A group of 1200 Russian prisoners were paraded around Germany in cattle trucks for several weeks with the word "Bolsheviks" painted on the outside. With no sanitary facilities, little food or water, starved and beaten many died on the way. When they were unloaded at the camp, many collapsed and died as they tried to struggle to the delousing showers. They were herded into barracks. In the morning the dead were carried out on pallets. Observed by Australians, including Jim who was there at the time, they were warned, "You feed them you are dead."[10]

A shocking experience, this must have hardened the Australians' attitude towards the Germans. However they had to cooperate with their captors in order to make life bearable. In the areas around Wolfsberg there were many labour camps and men were put to work building the railways and roads, which were repeatedly blown up by partisans. One group developed a unique routine for their day:

"We realised we could comfortably handle the replacement 90 meters of track each day provided we worked as a coordinated team. We kidded the German guards that we were flat out handling the 90 meters daily and gradually a work contract developed, the terms of which allowed for fewer meters being laid due to air raids and rain. If there were no interruptions we could lay the 90 meters before lunch, then relax in the sun or swim in the river."[11]

Red Cross delegate Dr. Descoeudres, visits the worksite of a detachment based at Wolfsberg Stalag 18A. Photo Red Cross

For the men in Stalag 18A the conditions were at times pleasant enough as far as being a POW could be. However "Barbed Wire Fever" had to be kept at bay and it was well known that the Australians had a talent for cooperation and organised fun. Wolfsberg had an extensive library and older men were able to offer classes in different subjects such as physics, math, psychology and agriculture. In the British library there were nearly 15000 books. There were also theatre entertainments and a French and British orchestra, along with playing cards and footballs to keep the men occupied.[12]

However towards the end of the war things became pretty dire, as the ability of the camp authorities to access proper supplies declined and the machinery of the Reich collapsed. The men knew the war was nearing an end and often looked to the sky as it went dark from the huge formations of American bombers heading into the Reich. In December 1944 the Camp was bombed by USAF. The British Surgery and Chapel were destroyed, 61 POW's were killed along with the chief British doctor and several guards. The injured were taken to the local hospital and many lives were saved by the resident German surgeon.

The war in Europe was drawing to a close and the evacuations of Wolfsberg started in April 1945. The sick were sent away in railway carriages and many of the healthy began a futile journey on foot as the Red Army closed in from the North East and the British approached from the South. Fortunately for the POW's the Allies and the Russians had come to a formal agreement that each side would accommodate their liberated soldiers. There was mistrust between the two but it was in the interests of the Command of both armies, to do the right thing for the men that came into their protection. The Allies also managed to secure an agreement that there was to be no forced labour outside of the holding camps. The reality was though, that if one was not prepared to work then no food was provided.

Inside the camps men were relatively safe in contrast to the conditions of people on the roads, which were horrendously dangerous. A variety of groups including women and children refugees, ex POW's and soldiers from various forces mingled and clashed as they fled in conflicting directions. Food was particularly scarce and living off the land was a precarious business. There are terrible stories of forced labourers and refugees being herded by Germans towards the Reich, meeting between Australians fleeing in the opposite direction.

It became urgent for the Allied authorities to secure the safety of their prisoners as many were being brutally herded towards other camps deeper into German territory. Eventually they were able to formalise an agreement with the Nazi authorities that prisoners would be left where they were in the camps, provided they were not able to re-enter the war. This was unlikely except for a few who would have had important information. Most were in ill health and not able to contemplate anything more than liberation and food.

"On 01 May 1945 the British and Americans received assurances from the "Protecting Power" the Swiss Red Cross, that that prisoner movements had ceased, the bulk of the POW's collected were in the large Stalags and became open to visits from ICRC and the Protecting Power"[13]

Stalag 18 A was liberated on 08 May 1945 by five British soldiers who parachuted into a nearby field. The camp *Kommandant*, Captain Steiner, subsequently handed over his command to the Senior British Medical Officer and Men of Confidence of the various nationalities. A little later a conference of all nationalities took place. On the same day French and British inmates relieved their former guards of their arms and took control of the Armoury, the Post Office and the Railway Station. They also took complete control of the local Gendarmerie. After some of the men had taken their own personal record cards from the *Kommandantura*, the remainder were burnt.[14]

The nearby camp at Spittal was liberated by the Americans on a bombing raid with the payload being several hundred kilos of sweets, cigarettes and various food stuffs. The rejoicing was said to be indescribable.[15]

The feeling in Stalag18A was probably not too dissimilar as the men realised the war was finally over and that they would be going home. What a relief to have finally made it through the war. After all Jim had been through in the Tobruk battles, the Italian camps, cattle trucks, floating prisons and abusive guards and coping with wounds, he could at last have some real hope of going home. The hand-over in Stalag 18A was in marked contrast to many of the horrific stories about camps in Germany and their liberation. The men of both sides treated each other with respect and maintained their dignity. The privations of the war had not extinguished their sense of decency. After a few weeks they were sent to holding camps in Italy then on to the UK by sea or air. Was Jim "Pee Wee" Sedawie evacuated at this time? The evidence supports it as his service record notes: "25.5.45 Previously reported POW, now reported arrived UK ex western Europe"[16]

Credit must be given to the British as this took place all of seventeen days after the liberation of Stalag 18A. It seems that a high priority was placed on the rescue of POW's, probably for military as much as humanitarian grounds. In the case of the Australians, their country was still at war with the Japanese. Not that Jim would be going to new battles in the Pacific but some of the men from Europe would be needed back home.

A holding camp for the Aussies was set up at Eastbourne in southern England where they were welcomed as heroes and looked after with the best of care and hospitality. This must have been a pretty euphoric experience after the years of confinement, danger and risk. Three weeks after arriving in the UK Jim was granted "Proficiency Pay" and was able to travel about the UK on a free rail pass issued to all ex POW's and returned serviceman, but this was not for Jim as he was "Dying to get back to Aussie" as he had said in his letters on several occasions. Two days after receiving his pay the record shows that he "embarked UK for Australia 19.6.45."

And that he "disembarked in Fremantle 17.7.45. 17

For Pee Wee the war was over and he was back in his beloved "Aussie" but had yet to make it back to Ascot. Spending a month in Melbourne with his family he had a reunion with his brothers at a local pub. They were in the army at the time, however they had not seen combat the way he had. Suffering from "Bronchial Asthma", which we now know was a bullet fragment in his lung, he went AWOL and forfeited nine days pay. Feeling desperate, he was in and out of trouble with the Army and his condition must have been serious as it is mentioned five times before he is admitted to Greenslopes Military hospital, in Brisbane on the 29 September 1945.

Lying in a clean bed and being looked after in a hospital, after all he had been through must have been pretty overwhelming. The people in Brisbane he loved - Keith and his family - would have been overjoyed to hear news of him being back and to visit him in hospital. He was discharged, two weeks later on the 15 October. It was time to go home, recover and catch up on all the news of what had happened at Ascot during the war.

CHAPTER EIGHT

"THE REAL INVASION"

The big news was the "invasion" of the Americans. Before 1941 Brisbane was a sleepy town much like country Queensland. Infrastructure was undeveloped and most secondary roads were still dirt. Culturally the city was isolated and people were largely unaffected by events of the outside world. The beginning of the war in 1939 had little effect on the general population. Unless you had a relative or friend serving overseas the war was remote. Keith was among of the few people in Brisbane with a direct connection to the front - he was receiving letters from Pee Wee.

The 2/15th battalion had left Brisbane in December 1940 and had been overseas for exactly a year when the Americans arrived. Initially they were seen as saviours and that Australia now had a fighting chance against the Japanese. Better dressed, well spoken and generally regarded as polite, they were also much better paid than the average Australian soldier. As the famous saying went, "Over here, over-sexed and overpaid."

Brisbane was rapidly transformed from a sleepy backwater to a bustling and chaotic city. Men and machinery were being unloaded and transported around town, often at breakneck speeds, accompanied by a sharp increase in traffic accidents. In one incident an American soldier driving a loaded truck crashed headlong into a tram killing five people. There were soldiers everywhere making themselves known and being entertained by the local population. My mother, who was 13 at the time, remembers being visited by a US navy Captain. He gave the family a musical jug that played Alug Ansung, which I still have. She lived with her parents and sister, above their shop on Kingsford Drive, Hamilton, not far from Brett's Wharf and the ships at anchor. Her daily trip by tram to school to in the Valley would have taken in much military activity. However she did not want to talk about the war and said it was a bad time in her life. Some would say Brisbane didn't cope with the influx. The population went from 300,000 to 600,000 almost overnight.

As noted by Nelson Johnson an American Diplomat at the time:
"Brisbaners are being pursued around on their own streets, in their favourite eating places and out of their homes. Naturally they are uncomfortable, irritable and inhospitable with their invading hosts."[1]

Although there was social friction, just as many stories are told of great times together, sharing hard work and a vibrant social life. There is plenty of evidence of two forces and societies forming great bonds of friendship. The Courier mail reported on 01 Feb.1947, at the closing ceremony of the Eagle Farm facility:

"The US Consul (Mr. Peck), the G.O.C. Northern Command, Maj.-Gen. R H Nimmo, and Australian Government representatives were present. 'Good Friends' The commanding officer of the unit Captain F.W. Lucterhand said and the relationships formed between US servicemen and the people of Brisbane had been an important factor in cementing the excellent feeling between two great English-speaking democracies — America and Australia. Many friendships that last a lifetime had been formed. Like himself, many American servicemen had married Australian girls."[2]

Keith, who would have been at this ceremony, had many American mates and told tales of card games and drinking Johnny Walker Whiskey. As a young teetotaller he would not touch a drink, but one time he was tempted: "The last thing I can remember was pestering this Yankee for one more glass. The next thing I remember is waking up in hospital with alcohol poisoning. I never touched a spirit drink after that, only beer."

Almost every night Brisbane was a raging party town with queues to get into dance halls filled with wild jitterbugging and dancing and "necking" cavorting and fighting which went on till late. Queensland law at the time forbade the selling of alcohol in dance halls but this was often ignored as was the case at the Ritz dance hall as one reveller recalls:

"The tables were loaded with food and drink and as the night wore on it got noisier and louder. The sailors, officers and girlfriends were getting merry and some of them hopelessly drunk, so much so that young girls were passing out with too much drink and were being carried out to waiting taxi cabs to be driven home. That's when the brawls started."[3]

US style entertainment 1942. Photo. Peter Dunn's "Australia @ War"

The Trocadero was a swinging jazz club frequented by service people and civilians alike on the South Bank of the river. A favourite story Keith told was about the evening the celebrations got out of hand. As he recalled:

"It was closing time on Sunday and the owner was trying to get the soldiers to leave but he wasn't having much luck. This is when they started to break up the place and throw chairs. The manager got the band to keep playing and eventually got them to leave. They walked across the Victoria Bridge and up Queen St looking for beer. After kicking in several shop fronts on the way up the street they arrived at the Grand Central Hotel in Queen Street, not far from MacArthur's headquarters. They were about to kick in the plate glass doors when the publican, Frank Pfitzenmaier came out and confronted them.

"What do you want?'

"Beer!!" they said

He gave them two kegs, they said they needed taps. He gave them taps on the condition they would be brought back.

"We need glasses"

"I not giving you glasses."

So they went three doors down to a Greek cafe and took all the glasses they needed. They then rolled the barrels up to the steps of the Post office, a distance of about 60 meters. Here they sat on the stairs, drank the beer and threw the glasses onto the stone steps. They took the kegs and taps back the next day."

These were Australian soldiers and Keith was part of the group and, in his hand written notes the story is told in the first person. This would explain the amount of detail and the "tagging along effect" of how the episode is related. I was told that they were men who had come back from the war on leave. Brisbane was a small town and Keith some who might have been Pee Wee's mates.

The Trocadero where they had come from was on the south bank of the river not far from where the current Gallery of Modern Art stands today. It seems the South Bank was where a lot of the social action took place. At the time the US enforced strict segregation between the races especially in the Southern States and prejudice was common in the American Services. It must have seemed the natural thing to separate the American Negroes buy confining them to South Brisbane. They were safe there, but any who ventured into the city would be on the receiving end of a certain beating from the Provos and had the possibility of being shot. Segregation was rigidly enforced by US marshals.

109

It was an offence for Negroes to cross the Victoria bridge into the City. However it was quite permissible for white soldiers cross the other way.

With the arrival of thousands of "coloured" American Negro troops the authorities had a major problem with a clash of cultures. The official "White Australia Policy" prevented non Anglo European races from emigrating to the country. One solution was to send many to outback towns and remote places, working as labourers doing, heavy manual work such as building air fields and unloading cargo.

In March 1942, 6346 Negro troops arrived in Australia. One issue that seemed to cause the most consternation was the idea that white Australian girls, prostitutes even, would be made available to satisfy the "lust" of these Negroes. In certain circles this seemed to be an unthinkable state of affairs. This was another culture shock for Brisbane people, but many found that rather than being dangerous, African Americans were charming and often physically superior. Some were invited into homes and to dances. A Brisbane woman Pamela Davenport said:

"I had a very soft spot for the American Negroes. They were always so cheerful and I loved their smiles, so white against their polished black skin."[4]

It was also the case that American Negroes were often highly principled Christians and there were several Negro Choral groups that frequented Churches in the city. One led by Laurence Sims of Huston Texas was a favourite. There were also many popular American "Preachers" who were guest speakers at various churches, and some GI's would go absent without leave on Sunday mornings in order to attend church.[5]

While most GI's were sober law abiding citizens, the attention of history has focused on more colourful events. Some sections of the community were alarmed at what they saw as the breakdown of moral order in Brisbane. This was not without cause as activities such as drinking, partying, prostitution and gambling all increased rapidly in 1942. The police force of the day was virtually swamped by the increase in crime and black market activities. Some conservative sections of Queensland society, including the Catholic Archbishop of the day, Duhig, warned of the collapse of public morality.[6]

Conventional wisdom might have us believe that Brisbane before the war was a quiet and peaceful place and that the Americans were responsible for stirring up trouble. However a search of the Brisbane Courier Mail in the mid 1930's, just prior to the war reveals a more complex picture. On 07 December 1936 there were two fatal affrays at Brisbane city hotels. In one,, an invalid passer-by was viciously bashed about the head, falling onto a pile of timber and dying before the ambulance could arrive. The other was a woman who was stabbed by another woman with a scout knife, 200 yards from the previous incident. She bled to death in a taxi on the way to hospital. Both perpetrators were apprehended and charged with murder. The Courier Mail Archives from this period also reveals Brisbane, especially the City and nearby Hotels of Kangaroo point and South Brisbane to be somewhat dangerous and violent places. The financial hardship and high levels of unemployment of the depression era seem to have taken a toll on Brisbane society. The City had seen its fair share of trouble before 1941, but few would have been expecting what was to come.

On the 28 April 1940 the Courier Mail records that Brisbane police had to cope with a large influx of prostitutes from Sydney and Melbourne as a result of police efforts in those cities to clamp down on their activities. Many of these women were associated with criminal elements and were not welcome. The Police made strenuous efforts to prevent them from becoming established in the city as frequent brawls had broken out between these women and their associates. A major incident occurred in the city just a couple of months before the Americans arrived. Evidence seems to show that Brisbane was well and truly feeling war time pressures, before the Americans arrived.

The following article from the Courier Mail Monday 28 October 1940 sets the scene.

Five Hours Disturbance: EARLY CLOSING OF HOTELS OPPOSED

Civilians Involved in Brawls

Scenes unparalleled in the city's history were witnessed on Saturday night in a demonstration by soldiers and civilians which lasted over five hours. During the greater part of the night the soldiers were in charge of a small section of Queen Street. Hundreds of pounds worth of plate glass display windows and doors -in Queen-street and Edward-street hotels were smashed. "Stink bombs" were thrown and burst among hundreds of milling soldiers and civilians.

Trams were forcibly brought to a standstill with their trolley poles being torn from the overhead wires. A tramway official tried to stop a batch of men boarding a tram and a free-for- all fight developed in the front cabin, which was quickly vacated by the women passengers. Police jumped on the tram and after a struggle put the soldiers off.

Motor traffic had to be directed into Adelaide and Elizabeth streets. Many shops, including cafes, closed their doors when it became evident that the authorities could not handle the situation. Although practically every available member of the police force and a strong force of military pickets were powerless to stop the disturbance, they managed to confine it to that section of Queen-street between Edward and Albert streets.

During the height of the disturbance the rioters broke the glass of "call boxes" and the fire brigade turned out twice to false alarms. On the second occasion the fire engines had to plough their way through several thousand people in Queen Street."

Estelle Runcie remembers how in 1942 most of the early fighting was between different sections of the Australian forces, the Air Force and Army being rivals. She recalls walking home from work and seeing a large group of men milling about on Queen St at North Quay all fighting. People were standing around watching and it was Army vs Air Force, there were no Americans involved.[7]

Seventy years later it is hard to imagine the culture and atmosphere that the American Serviceman would have to merge into. Nothing could have prepared Brisbane for December 1941. If the authorities were challenged by difficult and sometimes violent behaviour previously, the effect of hundreds of thousands of American soldiers on the already growing population of resident Australian military personnel, was about to push the city's slow pace and somewhat orderly way of life over the edge.

The Queensland Government had to come to terms with a sharp increase in demand for the services of prostitutes. Establishments such as *Elsie's* in Albert St City, *Killarney* in Fish Lane South Brisbane and two others behind the Breakfast Creek Hotel catered for the insatiable desires of men about to be sent to the front, uncertain if they would ever return. Reports have said that in those days men would wait in line for their three minute turn, which cost one pound - four days pay for an Australian soldier.[8]

The Yankee soldier was able to show the average Brisbane girl a good time, in a way not possible for their Australian counterpart. They had access to ice cream, alcohol, cigarettes, nylon stockings and other luxury goods at comparatively low prices from their PX canteen on the corner of Adelaide Street and Creek Streets. Largely unavailable to Australian soldiers, these goods were being rationed in Australia. Along with American customs such as caressing women in public and a more formally polite way of interacting, jealousy and resentment became common among Australian men. Considerable tension built up between the forces and fist fights were common. The Courier Mail paints a vivid picture.

FIGHTING OVER MEN

"Casualties" at Dances

Rival gangs of young women seeking the attentions of men of the fighting forces, have started a strange gang war in Brisbane. Almost every night some young woman is given first aid for injuries received in a brawl at one or other of the city's dance halls frequented by soldiers and sailors. Two of the best black eyes seen in Brisbane decorated a young woman who had been accused by another girl of "pirating" her soldier friend. Generally, however, the injuries are not so severe, and mostly the victims are treated for lacerations and contusions. Many torn frocks have been testimony to the viciousness of the brawls. Like most arguments between women, the feud shows signs of spreading and men in the fighting forces are finding they are being drawn into a squabble which, although it concerns them, is not of their making.[9]

Keith recalls at the Wintergarden, in Queen Street going to the pictures with two girl friends at when a fight broke in the foyer. He said:

"The fight had only been on a few minutes when some American MPs showed up. They just waded in and hit this bloke over the head and he fell on the ground. I was with a couple of girls; we were shocked at what they had done."

I always enjoyed a favourite Christmas story of my uncle Louie Pfitzenmaier whose father was the Publican at the Grand Central Hotel in Queen Street. The Grand Central was one of the main hotels at the time and the scene of much revelry. He recalls:

"One day when Dad was in the bar of the hotel a couple of American MPs came in and said:

"Mr. Pfitzenmaier, if you have any trouble with our men just ring this number",

"They handed me a small strip of paper with a phone number on it. I stuck it on the wall in the bar. Sure enough when a fight broke out with Americans involved, I rang the number and pretty quickly the MPs would turn up. The foot path was crowded and would they use their batons on the passers-by just to get into the hotel. No questions were asked, they would just push in, use their batons and break up the fight. Paddy wagons were waiting out front and the culprits were dragged away."

**American MPs outside the Grand Central 1942.
Photo. John Oxley Library, State Library Qld.105718
Note the metal protection grills over the front windows.**

"The American provost Marshall reported that in October 1942, they were breaking up about 20 brawls per night, and American soldiers were being rolled by their Australian counterparts. As Neville Smith of the Melbourne Argus noted: "Brisbane was youthful and brimming with the energy of the superbly fit.' While the official historian, Gavin Long noted, Brisbane had become "barbarous" and was one of the most vivid places in the Southern Hemisphere.[10]

The Historical Record sheds light on the fact that brawling, involving service men of both nations, as well as civilian men and women, was common, widespread and often violent. It reached a climax on Thanksgiving Day 26th November 1942, with what has been called, The Battle of Brisbane. But before we get to that, we have to catch up with Keith at the ship yard.

CHAPTER NINE

KANGAROO POINT

During the war Keith worked at the Kangaroo Point Ship yard. Today the district is a very expensive inner city suburb, with lots of high rise apartments with spectacular views of the city and the Story Bridge. Still a ship yard till the early 1980's, it was finally redeveloped and appropriately called "Dockside" with some units being built looking over the flooded dry dock. It has a unique place in the history of Brisbane and used to be an important industrial centre. Keith went to work there in early 1942.

Soon after war broke out he was looking for a more consistent job than the Cold Stores. His dad, John, was a friend of Mr. Arthur Deakin who owned the Evans Deakin ship yard and engineering works at Kangaroo Point. Mr. Deakin lived in a "big flash house" on the hill in Windermere Road not far from Dobson Street, off Racecourse Road - the very same hill he had raced down in his billy cart only a few years earlier. Here he recalls a visit to the "flash house".

"Dad, (Keith's father John) said "You go and tell Mr. Deakin that you're my son and see if he'll give you a job." "Who's MR. Deakin?" I asked. "So I went round to his house and saw him and he said "Any son of John's will get a job with me. You go down to Evans Deakin shipyard." Mr. Deakin said.

"Where's that Mr. Deakin? "

"At Kangaroo Point, you go in there tomorrow and tell them I sent you and they will give you a job."

"So I went there and had a look around, 200 bloody blokes everywhere. They were building Corvettes, one down from a Destroyer. I went down there and saw Mr. Brown the foreman, a boiler man, top class bloody bloke. They only had one crane and were building a second one as fast as they could. They were building the ship's plates at Rocklea and sending them down on trucks by Jacksons the carriers. They were skidded off the truck. We had to get them off the skids with a block and tackle, eight of us, pull yer guts out, bloody inch plate for the keel, bloody hard work but I didn't mind it, I was fit."

Later Mr. Brown said, "I've got an easier job for you."

I used to tell dad what was going on at home, so maybe this came through Deakin. Hard yakka but I used to clean up and go out to a dance at night and I was a strict teetotaler.

"Come on I've got a job for you, come and I'll show you. That mans gonna heat those rivets up in that oven over there." Said Mr. Brown.

"The riveting crew didn't have an old hand blower like at Kelly's blacksmith. They would heat the rivet up white hot with a pair of tongs, in a furnace, a bloke on the other side would hold it up with a big block and then the bloke on the outside had a gun, Brrrrrt, the rivet went in."

This went on for a while then Mr. Brown said to me,

"I want you to go and see that foreman there, he's got some money for you."

"Unknown to me you got as much as a squad leader, a riveter, a holder upper, a passer and a cook. We were getting paid bonuses by the Government for putting in so many rivets per day. It depended on where they were, on the bottom they were big heavy rivets, little teck rivets on the deck, where you might put in 300 a day. A fella would come round with a chalk and mark them off. You'd get five to six pound extra per week."

Riveting the deck plates Kangaroo Point 1943. Photo. AWM 059865

This seemed quite a lot of money especially if one pound was four days pay for an Australian soldier.

"Six days a week, twelve hours a day, I worked there for about eighteen months. We all worked in harmony, there were no fights. A young bloke was the billy boy and he used to light a big fire and boil all the billy's for *smoko* 15 – 30 billies at a time. No cameras were allowed and we used to play dice for half an hour after work. It was hard work and I got tired but I didn't mind, it was for the war effort."

Then there is the story of the River Burdekin, the biggest ship Evans Deakin had built at that stage, Keith recalls:

"One day an order came through for some big cargo ships and they had to move some houses. "Out ya bloody get, there's a war to be fought!"

This was a cargo ship called the "River Burdekin" a "River Class" ship that was famous for a near disaster when it was launched. They were built up to the deck level in the dry dock then launched into the river backwards."

The River Burdekin was commissioned by the Australian Government and built by Evans Deakin in 1943. It was a steam powered cargo vessel of 5,108 gross tons, length 449' 8" (136m) The steam engine and boilers were built by Evans Deakin in their Brisbane plant at Archerfield.

The River Burdekin: Photo John E Hoskin Flotilla-Australia

On the day of the launch there were several hundred dignitaries, guests and workers watching. The VIP's were on a temporary wooden podium. There was also a brass band playing, "Pom Pom Pom." As the ship slid down the massive cradle of wooden beams, the section made of pine gave way and was crushed onto the hardwood beams underneath. Huge clouds of smoke billowed from the wood as the friction generated enormous heat. As part of the cradle collapsed, the ship jammed on the slipway and came to a halt with its stern half in the water and the bow still in the dock on the cradle. Everyone panicked, if the ship had come too far off the gantry the spectators would have been crushed. It came to rest with its stern suspended over the water. All were concerned it might split in half when the tide went out.

Two tugs were called and the biggest steam compressor in Brisbane was mounted against the bow. They tried to pull her off the cradle but it would not budge. The tide eventually went out but the ship didn't crack, they welded two massive RSJ's - steel beams - across the deck and it sat like this for weeks till she was eventually raised high enough for a new cradle to be inserted. Men bashed with sledge hammers to force wooden wedges between the hull and the wooden beams. For some time a loud "pinging" sound could be heard for a long way off. When it came to launch, three tugs were attached to the stern and the steam compressor was mounted at the bow. It released suddenly and floated into the river. The driver of one of the tugs panicked and thought he was going to be rammed. His large tow rope had caught around his propeller and he drifted down river. She was eventually fitted out at the nearby docks.

In Jim's letter from the front, in August 1941, he mentions a ship Keith is building,

"Well Keith I was pleased to know that you are working and getting good money and see if you can hang on there till I get back and then you and I will go in for some sort of business, I wish you were just finishing the boat that was going to bring me back to Aussie, as this place is making an old man of me,"

Keith recalls,

"We worked flat out to get this thing built. It was a big 10,000 ton cargo ship, the same as the ones the yanks were building in the States, only they were welding theirs and we were riveting ours, they used to launch theirs sideways and ours would be launched backwards.

The Yanks had a big production line, but some of them would split in half. Dad told me about the one that ran onto a sand bar in Morton Bay and broke open. It must have been a hospital ship as there were bandages and hospital gear floating in the river for weeks.

Records show this was the SS Rufus which ran aground on a sand bar in Morton bay in July 1942. The "Liberty Ships" were built by the hundreds in US shipyards. Manufactured in parts, they were assembled one every 3 days and had a reputation for splitting in half. As was the case of the SS Rufus which came apart on a sand bar north of Stradbroke Island. The accompanying photo shows smoke still coming from a chimney, and people on the rear deck. However several thousand were built and became the backbone of American logistical support in the Pacific. Everything from planes to coffee to airstrip bitumen was unloaded from liberty ships at Brett's Wharf.

SS. Rufus off Stradbroke Island. Photo AWM. 305441

Some Brisbane residents may be surprised to know that the city was the base for South West Pacific American Submarine fleet. We were one of the only ports in the region that had a dry dock capable of taking ships this size. Sixty six submarines were based in Brisbane. At New Farm wharf two tender ships were anchored where subs would arrive for maintenance and repairs. There were barracks for the men and supplies in the wharf buildings. By 1943 the facility was fully operational and able carryout complete overhauls of submarines.[1]

Submarine base New Farm, The USS Albacore, 4th from left. Photo Courtesy Boolarong Books

There are several stories of Submarines having mishaps with the Japanese Navy and then making their way to Brisbane for repairs. Two of the most interesting were the USS Albacore and the USS Growler. The Albacore, a Gato class submarine, visited 3 times for repairs and In November 1943 the, was involved in dramatic battles with the Japanese Navy and other US ships and was credited with sinking the cruiser Tenryu. At one point she was accidently attacked by US aircraft dropping depth charges and later was damaged by Japanese depth charges, causing her to run for Brisbane.

As Keith tells the story, he was working at Evans Deakin, when a call was made for volunteers to go to the Dry dock at South Brisbane to work on a sub. The Albacore had radioed ahead and was heading across the Pacific south of Japanese activity, but being damaged it had to travel on the surface. It was soon realised that the Albacore was going to be too long to fit in the dock. It seems laughable today, but a team of men were sent with jack hammers to lengthen the dock as the ship sailed toward Brisbane. Keith continues the story:

"Some bloke from the Government came round and said,

"This is gonna take too long, we have do to something else."

"Well the next day they decide to blast the rock out, boom boom. Well you shoulda' seen it, they cleared the area and boulders were landing up on Grey St."

Some years ago I visited the dry dock with Keith and inspected the site of the blast. Most of the dock is lined with large bricks, but the last section is jagged rock. A tell tale sign.

Keith recalls:
"I was told that a message was sent to Brisbane from Pearl Harbour that the USS Albacore could not submerge and they wanted to send it to Brisbane for repairs in a hurry. I volunteered and went to the dry dock at South Brisbane. There we worked 12 hr shifts for six weeks, six days a week. I worked as a "holder upper". We had to hold the rivet in place while it was hammered from the other side. Anyway we worked flat out for six weeks repairing the ship. I was on the riveting crew."

The Albacore was credited with sinking the most tonnage of Japanese ships by a US submarine and she received four Presidential Unit Citations and nine battle stars for her service.

The story of the USS Growler is a unique chapter in the history of maritime Australia. A large mural at the Brisbane Maritime Museum at South Brisbane, adjoining the dry dock, celebrates this incident. Like the Albacore, the Growler was damaged in a confrontation with a Japanese freighter, which tried to ram the sub, but the quick action of the Captain resulted in the sub changing course and ramming the Japanese boat, sinking it. Although the bow of the Growler was bent to one side, it could still submerge and the Captain's last order was to "Take Her Down". He made his men go into the ship, while he remained on the bridge, wounded by machine gun fire as she went down. He received the US Medal of valor and the Growler sailed to Brisbane without its Captain. Here a new bow, designed by Clem Jones, former mayor of Brisbane was manufactured by Evans Deakin at Archerfield and fitted at the dry dock. Welded on both sides of the new bow was a steel kangaroo, with the Growler being nicknamed "The Kangaroo Express". It went back to service in the Pacific.

US Submarine at New Farm, Photo Boolarong Books

During the war the skies of Brisbane were filled with the noise and sights of American and Australian aircraft. Keith recalls:

"Working at the shipyard we often saw close up, planes flying overhead, Yankee dive bombers would practice dive bombing the ships in the yard. They would fly under the Story Bridge, pull up and buzz the ships. One day this pilot clipped the top of a mast of a ship at Brett's Wharf at Hamilton, he lost control and crashed on the Army Depot at Meendah and killed a cook. Just so the Yanks couldn't get the better of them, some Aussies flew a medium bomber, a Marauder, under the bridge. I saw it coming in from over the city and they were going, "whoosh", and they were gone!"

If you have not had the pleasure of riding the Brisbane City Cat ferry under the bridge, I highly recommend this "voyage" so to speak. It helps bring to life the daring of these pilots. It's not a very big space for planes at high speed.

Story Bridge Photo. Author

Dad also said that at any one time the river was congested with boats coming and going. Once an American destroyer went up river past Hamilton too fast and the bow wave smashed a lot of small wooden jetties. There was "a hell of a commotion." The Old Man worked at the yard for about eighteen months and kept his gate pass.

He must have had enough of this back breaking work. Leaving, he got a new job with the Americans at the Eagle Farm. But on Thanksgiving Day 1942 he was working at the yard, a short walk into town.

CHAPTER TEN

THE BATTLE OF BRISBANE

Thanksgiving Day 1942, became a day of mayhem and bloodshed on the City streets of Brisbane when a group of Australian soldiers became involved in a dispute with American Military Police. There are many stories and rumours about what happened that night and the details are more closely examined by other authors, notably Thompson and Macklin in "The Battle of Brisbane", 2000. Keith was there that night and his recollections are part of my childhood memories and so this is an important chapter in the history of Brisbane and the O'Neill family.

Keith was in the VDC, the Volunteer Defence Corp. Originally marching in Ascot State School yard with broom sticks in 1939, he had volunteered for overseas service several times but was required to stay with his jobs in the shipyard and airport. How he found the energy to go into town at night dancing is beyond me, but he was young and fit and everyone else was there too.

He recalls:
"I used to wear my VDC uniform and that would get me into the army dances. I would go into town nearly every night after work. I was there the night of the Battle of Brisbane and saw the riot. A Yank sentry shot an Aussie in the Eagers Building (American Canteen) and all Yank Leave was cancelled for the next night but there were still many fights. They smashed each other all over town. At one stage there was a double line of Yankee Naval Patrol with fixed bayonets

outside the Roma St. Police station to stop men trying to get at the weapons inside."

The American Army PX Canteen was on the corner of Creek and Adelaide St. The Red Cross canteen was across the road and the Australian Canteen a short distance away. Due to their proximity, this area was almost always crowded with men from both services. In town that night a couple of Australian soldiers were with an American friend and they had had a few drinks. Private James Stein of the US 404 Signals was invited to the Australian PX canteen for a Thanksgiving Day drink with his Australian mates. They bumped into some other Aussies in the doorway of the canteen, a minor scuffle ensued that attracted the attention of two American Provos. Some other soldiers came out of the Australian Canteen to see what the fuss was about. At some point one of the Provos laid his baton across the head of an Australian. A melee ensued and the Provo was knocked to the ground and kicked. Australians' unique attitude to authority is somewhat different to that of the Americans. We are unlikely likely to defer to authority figures, especially if it seems they are being arrogant. Damien Parer, Australian war correspondent at the time had this to say:

"Those American MPs, those bloody bastards, they always hit first and talk later."[1]

This was regarded as very un-Australian and our troops hated the Provos, who they saw as provocative. It was later noted by official US war historian Dudley McCarthy:

"It is probably fair to say that in the United States the display of batons and firearms in the hands of police is an effective way of quelling a riot, whereas in Australia it is an effective way of starting one."[1]

And this is exactly what happened. The MPs were supported by other Provos who had witnessed the scuffle from their canteen entrance. They charged into the fray wielding their batons and managed to drag their semi conscious mate back into their

PX some fifty metres away. The Australians who had followed and gathered outside started calling for the cowardly American who had bashed their mate to come out. This had all taken place in the early evening after the Pubs had shut at 6pm and hundreds of soldiers were sent out of the bars onto the streets. At first the incident only involved a small group but by 7.15 PM there were about 100 Australian soldiers milling about, calling "come out and fight you bastards".[2]

By this time the crowd had swelled to about 500 and a wild melee ensued between American and Australian MPs, Brisbane police and Australian soldiers.

"Early In the brawl fire engines and the fire chief were called, and the crowd, expecting that the firemen were going to turn the hoses on them, broke quickly, but the firemen returned to the station."[3]

The local Police Inspector had called them hoping to quell the riot with water hoses but to his dismay the head fireman refused saying,

"My men are here to fight fires not quell riots."[4]

Police were called off leave from all stations and the Police Commissioner took charge. What ensued was an ugly riot where the soldiers began to throw rocks, traffic signs and other objects at the American canteen and the MP guarding the entrance. At this point the Americans called for assistance and reinforcements arrived quickly, including MP Norbet Grant who was armed with a loaded "riot" gun - a pump action shotgun. The appearance of the gun inflamed the crowd and some of them surged forward shouting,

"Put that fucking gun away"

To which Grant replied, "If you come any closer I'll have to shoot."

"The shooting occurred when soldiers rushed military police carrying riot guns while they were on duty outside the canteen."[5]

As the Aussies rushed him, Private Ed Webster grabbed the barrel of the gun and it discharged into his chest. He fell to the ground and later died of blood loss in the Royal Brisbane Hospital. Several others were treated for baton blows. In all three shots were fired and several soldiers were later treated for gunshot wounds. The crowd became enraged. There was a brief lull in the fighting while the injured Australians were carried away and the Australian Provos tried to calm the situation by mingling in the crowd without their MP identity armbands. A group of Australian Army pickets with unloaded rifles made an attempt to disperse the mob but most of them abandoned their helmets and rifles and joined in. Their rifles were snatched away by police or rioters. There was a large group of civilian police who had been called as back up but are reported to have not had much effect on the actions of the crowd.

The rioters were from the 2/9th battalion of the 7th Division who had recently returned from the Middle East and had seen action in New Guinea. As Lt. Watts of the 2nd Anti tank regiment said

"Those Yankee MPs picked on the wrong mob."[6]

After about three hours, the scene calmed down, the mob dispersed and a number of soldiers were taken into custody. However numerous other brawls took place that evening as Australians went looking for Yanks, many of whom were involved in brawls started as a result of the riot. How more were not killed is amazing, the police and authorities must have been in a panic. For some time after this the atmosphere in the City was tense and fighting was common.

As Keith said, the talk around town was,

"It was going to on for young and old."

He recalls that the next night there was fighting all over the city.

The Courier Mail of Monday 30 Nov, referring to the Friday 27 Nov. which was the day after the riot, says:

DISTURBANCES AMONG SERVICE MEN

BRISBANE, Sunday. Without assuming threatening proportions, disturbances again took place among service men in Brisbane on Friday night. The brawls were confined to individual fights. When place-names wore shouted by mob leaders, soldiers would quickly gather at the places shouted. Most of the soldiers gathered outside a canteen, where many-fights took place.

This level of disturbance went on in spite of a greatly increased security presence."

The report mentions a canteen and the fatal shooting and wounding. The general information about the riot is accurate but interestingly there is no mention of American or Australian soldiers. The story is in a small column with a total of 317 words. Censorship was strictly enforced at the time and this kind of disharmony between allies would have been used by the Japanese as propaganda if it had been widely published. However any one in Brisbane reading the story at the time would recognise the location and mention of a "canteen" and be able to place the incident as outside the American PX. And so the "Battle of Brisbane" entered into local folklore.

Four months later, the Courier Mail in March 1943 gives an account of the trial of some involved in the riot. With vivid descriptions and colourful language we receive an insight into the culture and attitudes of the time.

"Signalman J. A. Owens was charged with: — When on active service he committed a civil offence, that is to say, common assault, in that he, at Brisbane, in the vicinity of the U.S.A. Post Exchange, on November 26, assaulted Police Constable Nuendorf by striking him the head with a piece of wood. Owens faced five charges:

Constable Nuendorf, of Roma Street Police, said he heard Owens using much language during the disturbance. Owens was calling out,

'Come on - we will pull the place to pieces.'

He endeavoured to persuade the accused to go away and not be foolish. Owens replied: 'They hit one of our soldiers with a baton, and I'm not going.'

In evidence he said that he had been struck on the shoulder with a baton and he admitted to having cried out:

'Come here you mongrel, I'll have a go at you.'

The portrayal of the rioting varies between authors. Thompson & Macklin, go into minute detail in order to "set the record straight" as it were. Their detailed descriptions draw on many eye witness accounts, archival documents and the history of Brisbane. In "Yanks Down Under by Potts & Potts much of the detail agrees with Thompson & Macklin. One important point that Potts & Potts explain is:

"To a large extent it was an anti MP riot, Australians and Americans fighting MPs, rather than an inter Allied affair. It was not Aussies against Yanks or vice versa but both against Authority."[7]

This sentiment fits well with the general attitude towards American Provos who carried a baton and side arms and who were ready to hit first and ask questions later. Some authors play down the significance of the event and inter services conflict in general, claiming that other writers have been "sensation seeking" and that "brawls were unusual."[8]

There are also records that would reveal further insights into the culture of the time as the John Oxley Library in Brisbane holds several photos of American servicemen charged and or convicted of various offences. These include sexual assault, one case of murder, assault, theft and other offences of disturbance. Many Australian soldiers were charged with offences ending up in Boggo Road jail. Some were court marshalled and most released at the end of the war. Reporting for the "Tele", the evening paper, in those days would have been a colourful experience to say the least.

American Soldier Charged with assault 1944. Brisbane Telegraph. Photo: John Oxley Library, State Library Qld. 106124

After considering a range of works on this topic, extensive reading of the Courier Mail from the mid 1930's to 1943, and family eyewitness accounts, I would say that far from unusual, brawls were common. This is illustrated by the routine nature of the following brief article in the Sunday Mail 12th July 1942.

SAILOR INJURED IN CITY BRAWL

Brawls involving servicemen and civilians were numerous in the city again last night. Service and civil police quelled the disturbances. Ambulance men treated many minor injuries. One sailor who was injured at Victoria Place, South Brisbane, was taken to hospital.

Brawling was a part of Brisbane culture before the Americans arrived. As we have seen during the 1930's there were large camps of unemployed men in and around Brisbane, and with boredom, lack of work and women folk, it is not hard to imagine frustrations boiling over. So when thousands of soldiers, many of them intoxicated, began to mill about in town, the combination of competition for woman folk and issues of unequal pay and privileges, fighting was inevitable. The tensions in men returning from battle or about to be sent to the front must have been enormous and fighting was a way of releasing this tension and expressing rivalry. As the bloke in the 2/13th said, when referring to some Italians in North Africa, "The police in Tel Aviv gave us a better fight then this." It also brings to mind the all in brawl the 2/15th had with the "Red Bands" while training in Darwin, and being complemented for their effort by their CO. This culture of soldiers fighting is an interesting topic which in itself could be studied in more depth.

The Brisbane Authorities at times lost control of the situation and struggled to maintain a sense of order in the city, this is unsurprising as they had a war to fight and the threat of invasion hanging over their heads. Resources were stretched and tempers frayed in ways contemporary society has never had to deal with. A picture emerges of a city in chaos at times, with the social fabric stretched to the limit. What a young Keith O'Neill was living through, when he was twenty years old must have had a profound impact. Whether at the front or not, young men had to grow up quickly and face challenges unique to the times.

For Keith this also meant working long and difficult hours in war related industries. He had been getting a man days pay for a man's work since he was sixteen. The "Manpower Act" had kept him in Australia and he was "earning good money" as Pee Wee had mentioned in his letter. Such are the fortunes of war that some people benefited from the economic impact of military spending and a war time economy. Keith had volunteered three times to join the Army and Air Force. It was with a clear conscience that he stayed at home and worked throughout the war, developing skills and growing quickly from a youth of sixteen to a man with worldly knowledge. Brisbane was full of Americans and the next chapter of Keith's war brought him right into the belly of their military machine.

CHAPTER ELEVEN

KEEP THE WAR QUIET: EAGLE FARM

In January 1942 the decision was made to develop the then small landing field at Eagle Farm into the main air base for Brisbane. After working at the shipyard Keith went to work at the "Test Stands". The airport was also the Allison Engine test facility where maintenance was conducted and engines were tested before being refitted to a plane. By this time Keith had saved enough money to buy a 1927 "Chev 4". He had always been mad keen on cars, ever since he was the photo delivery boy with the pictures of the new cars on his bedroom wall. Once when he took his car to the Ascot Garage his mate Cyril Smith the mechanic asked,

"Have you been putting aviation fuel in this thing because the rings are all burnt out?"

"Well I had to stop doing that as it was ruining my engine."

Archerfield was the main Brisbane airport when the American fleet arrived, but it soon became inadequate. Eagle Farm, which was only about 2 kilometres away from the wharf, was to become a major staging post for Allied military aircraft. Planes unloaded at Hamilton in crates, were driven to the air field and assembled ready for the Pacific theatre. Aircraft would also come in from the battles further north, their engines were taken to the Allison assembly plant at Albion, a few kilometres away, where they would be reconditioned before being transported back to Eagle Farm. Here they were placed on an open air stand on the edge of the airfield and run for up to 5 hours at the red line to ensure they were safe.

Keith & Chev 4 & The Ascot Garage, Racecourse Road, Photos, O'Neill Collection & John Oxley Library, State Library QLD, 168774

Hooked up to a separate test panel with gauges and dials, the service man would to record the readings. If all was perfect the engine was reinstalled. If not ready it would be pulled down and re-examined.

Thousands of planes went through Eagle Farm: B17 Flying Fortresses, Liberators, Kittyhawks, Mustangs, Airacobras and Marauders, and Dad's favourite; the P38 Lighting. He recalls:

"One of my jobs was fitting the props. They had an electric motor in them so as to feather the prop. It had 14 studs and a network of brass wire. Holes were drilled around it and you had to lace the wire, it had to be tight. We had to work fast to get the engines off the stand and get the next one on. We were given a beautiful set of tools, chrome vanadium. At the finish they said we could keep them."

The strangest part of the story is that the residents of Brisbane complained about the noise. In the Courier Mail in August 1943 there appeared an article about the "Noisiest Job in the War". Keith kept a copy and It clearly shows a man in a hat, Keith, fitting the

Courier Mail Newspaper Cutting 13/8/43, O'Neill collection

prop. It had to be just right or the propeller might wobble and fly off at high speed. According to the original article a massive din was produced by six engines running full speed on open air stands. In order to stop the complaints, the Americans built two brick tunnels for the stands. As Keith recalled they were complaining from as far away as Redland Bay and Strathpine. The American Colonel at the time was heard to remark: "Don't they know there is a war to win?"

Keith working on an engine Photos. Peter Dunn Oz@War

The noise must have been incredible and it's a wonder he didn't go deaf at an earlier age. As the old man would say, "No ear-muffs in those days!"

At the Allison Overhaul Assembly Plant, just down the road at Albion was Edwin H. Oribin who was only 15 years old when he started there in around August 1942. He recalls: "On several occasions I went out to the GMH Allison Engine Testing Area at Eagle Farm Airfield and the noise and action out there was in stark contrast to the quiet efficiency of our Factory.

The engines were run with full size propellers, so they were mounted high above the ground. The reduction gear for the Airacobra engines was on a separate stand and was connected to the engine by a short 2 foot shaft. I went out there one day to retrieve a wrecked engine which had over-sped when the propeller and the reduction gear had parted from the shaft and took off and sailed over the fence into the bush just like a helicopter. It is believed that someone had forgotten to tighten the connecting bolts properly."[1]

Was the Old Man responsible for this? If so he didn't mention it. One can imagine work at the airfield was long, tiring and sometimes dangerous. Some incidents recalled by Keith include

"One day a Marauder, a medium bomber, just had its engines refitted but there was some doubt about whether it was ready for service. It was decided that it would be flown to Archerfield as a test. The plane took off, climbed into the air over the airfield, then flipped over and crash landed on its back and exploded."

The B26 Marauder was known a tricky aircraft to fly and early in the Pacific war got a reputation as a "widow maker", needing to be flown at exact speeds in takeoff and landing, it was prone to stalling and crashing when pilots flew at the wrong speeds. However design adjustments saw it go on to be a very effective aircraft. Between January 1943 and September 1945 at least 6 aircraft crashed at Eagle Farm.[3]

Hanger 7 built a distance away from the other hangers was the site for secret American testing of captured aircraft. Other ground crews knew about it but were not allowed to go there. Keith recalls:

"This day we were out in the open working on some engines when a Jap Zero came in really low. We all made a run for it as we thought it was an attack. As it turned out it was a Yankee pilot testing the Jap plane that had been captured up north."

Japanese Zero & Hanger 7. Photo Peter Dunn Oz@War

"Another time we watched a rebuilt zero being chased by a P38 Lightning and one time I saw a Kittyhawk do a belly landing."

It took me some time to figure out why Keith had such a high regard for the Americans as not everyone in Brisbane had good experiences with the visitors. There were many mixed feelings between Australians and their "invaders". However the Old Man's passionate belief in all things American was cemented on one fateful day working at the airfield. Keith recalls:

"In those days we used to clean our tools in aviation fuel. This evening I had been cleaning my tools in a half drum of fuel, I had high octane fuel on my overalls from the days work. It was wintertime and the boys used to warm themselves with fires in 44 gallon drums. After I finished cleaning I began to walk away when somehow a spark from a fire in a drum, ignited the fuel in my clothes and it blew up over me, setting me on fire. I raced about fifty yards to the mess hall where they were having dinner, yelling "Fire". My arms were burning as I ran in. I hit the swing doors and they came off the hinges. There were some big fire extinguishers there, monsters on a two wheel trolley. Whoosh - I was out in a flash. Within seconds some Yankees had put me out as I rolled on the floor of the canteen.

Eagle Farm Canteen 1942. Photo John Oxley Library, State Library Qld.156796

An ambulance came from Anne St in the City and it had to cross a railway line as there was no other way out and a train was being shunted on the track. The railway men kept the ambulance waiting for a long time before it was able to get through and there was an argument. The railway worker said: "Don't you know there's a war on?" to which they said "Don't you know a man's been burnt? 'After that I spent six weeks in hospital recovering from the burns. Eventually I returned to work at the stands. When I arrived back the crews had a poster on the wall and had taken up a collection for me."

Before the Americans arrived, Eagle Farm was a grass field with a few huts. In a remarkably short time it had grown into a world class airport. In February 1947 the last of the Americans left with a solemn flag lowering ceremony and many speeches about how successful the new airport had been.

"The Air Force unit at Eagle Farm had earned the reputation at higher headquarters of being one of the most efficient aircraft supply and maintenance units in the whole of the Pacific, he continued. The U.S. Air Corps would ever be grateful for the co-operation and assistance it had received from Australian civilians who had worked for it"[4]

While Keith was working at the airfield he was also manning a 3.7 inch anti aircraft gun which was stationed on the corner of Nudgee Rd & Gerler Rd. Hendra, a short distance from the airstrip. When not at the airfield he would be on the crew, manning the gun. In 1998 he was part of a ceremony in Brisbane where many of the men and women who served in vital industries during the war received the Civilian Service Medal 1939–45. The National Archives Fact sheet 39 records that,

"The Civilian Service Medal 1939–45 is available to those who served in a civilian organisation were required to work in arduous circumstances, and were subjected to military style arrangements and conditions of service."

The Old Man certainly worked under arduous conditions and in some danger. He earned the medal. After the war he went back to working at the cold stores, but his experiences at the ship yard and airport had changed him. Having developed new confidence in his abilities he would put them to good use in the post war economic expansion of Brisbane.

CHAPTER TWELVE

PEACE AND PROSPERITY

As we have head from Alison Flaherty the end of the war was a time of great celebration. A weight had been lifted from the nation. However not all were able to celebrate to the same extent. For those who had seen battle and ex POW's the war's end would have been a great relief but struggles with poor health and trauma were the experience of many returnees.

Pee Wee was not well when he returned. His record shows he had bronchial asthma, however as Keith and his cousin have said, he had a piece of shrapnel in his lung and they couldn't operate. Photos of Jim after the war show a different man to the one who had left Australia in 1940. He was discharged on medical grounds on 02 November 1945 and given nine days pay. He would have then gone on to a war service pension. In Jim's letter from Tobruk October 1941 he says:

"Well Keith I was pleased to know that you are working and getting good money, and see if you can hang on their till I get back, then you and I will go in for some sort of business."

That business turned out to be a fish run. You were supposed to go through the Fish Board, but Jim knew a fisherman and although you weren't supposed to, he would sell Jim fish. He and Keith would meet him at his boat on the river bank where Crescent Road meets Kingsford Smith Drive. At night they would load up with fresh fish buy hauling them up in baskets. They had a run around Highgate Hill, one around Bulimba and one around Hawthorne Park. Jim built the box to go on the trailer, with ice in it. He built up the run with a Chevy 4 before he had the Jeep. How he managed this is beyond me.

Remarkably Jim, Keith, Gladys and Keith's Mum Cornelia, made a trip to Melbourne in the Jeep. I don't recall much detail but here is a photo with the details on the back.

Jim returned to his beloved "watering hole" the Hamilton pub and caught up with old mates. Unfortunately there is not much to tell about this time but there is a couple of photos.

Jim & Norm Douglas (despatch rider) at the "Hammo" post war. Photo. O'Neill Collection

Rationing and shortages were around for some years. Frugality was the order of the day and essential goods such as petrol, butter and meat were rationed. You were given your allotted set of ration tickets for the month and when that ran out you didn't get any more. Us younger

**Jim his dog and mates Greenslopes Military Hospital Post War.
Photo O'Neill Collection**

Australians, with our long period of prosperity and high standards of living have little if any any conception of what life was like in those days. The country had been through almost two decades of financial hardship, depression and war. But by the later 1940's, things began to recover. However restrictions seemed to be mere challenges to Keith. He would find a way around them and he approached his post war financial endeavours with great gusto After Eagle Farm, Keith became a "truckie". He recalls:

"I bought an old truck off Wally Gibson on time payment and I linked up with a fella named Horsy Johns who was dealing in scrap metal. Iron and steel was in short supply and we would go to remote properties in South Western Queensland to collect scrap metal. Horsy was in the lead car, he would go to properties and approach the owners to see if they had any old cars or scrap iron laying about. Together we would load up the truck and take it to the nearest rail head which could be many miles away. The train took it to Brisbane and we sold it to the scrap merchants. One time I got bogged in the middle of nowhere and had to walk a day and half a night to a property to get someone to help."

Often there were problems starting the old truck and great frustrations were had with the crank handle.

"Yes in those days no starter motors, you had to 'wind her over'. This would sometimes lead to boiling point and one day I threw the crank handle as far as possible, landing in some long grass, lost. That didn't help but, I realised I needed a new truck."

But there were none to be had. Keith went into the Ford showroom in Newstead but was told he could join the waiting list for up to a year and a half. To counter this he would drop by each week and happily ask:
"Where's my new truck?"
He got his new Ford in six months and never looked back, eventually owning a fleet of 7 trucks, two tractors, bulldozers and various other equipment, plus industrial land with storage sheds. The skills he had picked up from the Americans were what provided the platform for his success. Efficiency, a sense of urgency to get things done, an amazing work ethic and a willingness to have a go, drove the Old Man. He must have been a dynamo in those days. He would go out to the back of Red Bank, a suburb of Brisbane, out in the bush and shovel on a load of garden soil. Here he recalls:

"I haven't told you this bit before but it all comes back. I'll tell you how I first started. I bought this first truck, a Ford and Stewey Kelly built the body on it. It was a wooden body with drop sides. So OK I didn't have the contract at the gas works then, you just went in. I'd get you a load of ashes, soil or manure or if you wanted, I'd get you a load of feathers, I would get anything.

We didn't have a phone at the time and had only second hand phone calls, you can imagine, Mum and Mrs. O'Dywer having a barney over the phone calls. Ah! Bloody hell it was great fun! They weren't fair dinkum cause they were great mates. She's three doors down, you'd ring her up and want a load of ashes - "When can ya give it to me?"

"Oh I dunno tomorrow, or sometime in the next week or so." Mrs.O'Dwyer would say:

"Bloody hell! After a month of that I said to mum we had to get a phone on."

"It was the winter of 1949. I'd been carting about six months and here around southern Queensland and Northern New South Wales was flooded, six weeks consecutive rain, the wipers never stopped. And of course after about two weeks of it the rail bridge at Kempsey got washed out. That was the main link to Sydney.

Well, in those day the Golden Circle cannery was called the C.O.D and was in the same place but not as big as it is today. Green grocers would go down there to get supplies. They usually had the rail to cart stuff away, but it's piling up and they can't move it fast enough. Well it's piling up. And there had to be free trade between the states, no tax. You had to get a permit and all this sort of drama if you wanted to sell interstate.

The fruit and vegies are staring to rot up here and Sydney are screaming their heads off. "We can't get any!" Well the Government can do it when they want to. So it was no weighbridges, no scales, no road tax, no permits, nothing, just go! Down to the cannery, load up and from there and take the load to Sydney. You would be given a special ticket to present to the C.O.D in Sydney. It entitled you to a load at Union Steel, BHP steel plate or a load of tin plate, and oh everything. This guaranteed you a load back! Cause a lot of people would get a load down and then chase all around Sydney to get a load back. If you got a slip you just went and your load would be waiting."

"The first trip, the load was that bloody high there was a bridge near Warwick I couldn't get under. I got beans and peas, it's a 5 ton truck and I've got 7 ton 3 on it. Piling it on and it was dark before I left. Getting near Warwick a bloke flags me down. "You won't get under that bridge with that load." He said "There is a detour road back there, pretty rough though."

At the COD Sydney, approx 1948. Photo O'Neill Collection

Well tip trucks had under-body hoists in those days and the weight just held it there. Well I'm a rookie and I'm lucky I didn't lose the bloody lot. I dropped down in a hole, bang! Well I took that load down and brought one back and did a few more. Yeah, six consecutive weeks it rained. The exhibition! They weren't going to hold the exhibition, the whole area was flooded. The main ring was flooded. But somebody got the bright idea the - "We'll dig it all up an put new drains down and put down decomposed granite." So they did this and the exhibition went on. And the rain, boy oh boy!

"Yes and I did six consecutive trips. I'd leave first thing Monday morning. I've never taken a drug in my life, I know a lot of blokes who were, take'n some kind of pills to keep them awake. I met a bloke in a café once who asked me: "Ya taken anything for it."

"Nope" I said.

"He didn't offer me any. I used to get to just this side of Newcastle, first thing in the morning. Me and a dozen other blokes would be there. I didn't know all the garages that were open 24 hours. There was only one open every pancake Thursday. You would get in and sometimes have to wait an hour before he'd open up. No sleeper cabs, just lie on the front seat and have a snooze. I'd get down there on the Tuesday morning, book into a hotel at Broadway, have a clean up, then go round to the C.O.D and get rid of the load. Get the chit, get another load on, by this time it was Thursday night. I'd get away Friday morning, get into the C.O.D, they were open 24 hours a day in those days. Get another load and go home. Mum would be at me: "You better go to bed!"

"No no! Why" "I said" There is a game of football on."

"I had helped to build the field before I was on this caper. That's right, the Saturday I would get back to Brisbane, grease the truck and get rid of it, crash the Saturday night, Sunday morning up early, take the tents down to the field. We didn't have any dressing sheds, a tent for the players and a tent for the visitors. Then go round to the Hamilton pub. The publican was the president of the licensed Victuallers Associations. This is where all the "Hamilton Heroes" would drink, bloody gold mine for him.

"Take as much beer as you like and bring back what you don't sell." he would say."

"And my truck had a big amplifier, connected up with a megaphone on the side for the announcements. Then when the game was over I would dismantle all the stuff, then go and have about half a dozen beers and crash. Then Monday down to the C.O.D. Six weeks I did that for. I was tired but I was fit and I wasn't playin' football then. I was about 27."

"When Adam Played Fullback for Hamilton", was one of the Old Man's favourite sayings, and adaptation of "When Adam had shorts," i.e. a time long ago when the biblical character was just a boy. Dad and his mates actually built the Hamilton Football Field from a piece of boggy waste ground on the corner of Kingsford Smith Drive and Nudgee Road, Eagle Farm. There are several photos of the men and boys with rakes and shovels spreading soil on the field.

At one point Keith was able to borrow a bulldozer off his mate Les Thiess, later Sir Leslie Thiess, who owned an earth moving business in those days. One Sunday morning they noticed that it was parked in another field not far away, so someone went and made a phone call asking if they could use it for the day. That turned out to be no problem and so much faster progress was made. It was low lying ground and one day before a game it was covered in water, so the men went around with crowbars and put lots of little holes over the field which made it drain off enough to let the next day's game go ahead. They had great fun and the photo of the crew in their XXXX beer sacks is a classic. I don't think Jim played football but he was part of the gang. The field is still there and the goal posts were only taken down in the 1990's. If Keith was 27 it was 1949, 4 years after the war.

**Hamilton Football Club 1947. Keith 5th from right, back.
Jim far right front.**

Keith had a wide circle of friends and they used to go on trips to the Gold Coast, Brunswick Heads and the Brisbane hinterland. Many a picnic was had at Cash's Crossing and other untouched bush camping sites that are now part of Brisbane suburbia. They would often get about fifteen or twenty on the back of the truck and head out for the day. No seat belts no police, no worries. Sometimes a dozen or so push bikes would be tied on.

As he got a bit older a favourite watering hole was the Brighton Hotel, today an ugly box, in those days a classic white two story Queenslander with verandas and a beer garden. We would sometimes go as a family for fish and chips on a Friday night.

The Gang, late 1940's Photos O'Neill Collection

Brisbane homes at the time had gas supplied to the door by two gas works, one at South Brisbane and one at Newstead. The Newstead gas works, a short drive from Ascot, used coal, which was "cooked" to make gas for heating. The left over waste material was called "breeze" a fine coarse black material, and it had to be carted away. In the early days men would go to the gas works and line up with their trucks waiting for a load. The operation was run by the manager. If you got there early and got a load you would usually have time to deliver it and come back for another. It was "first in best dressed" as Dad would say. The result of this process was that fights and arguments would develop and the manager would have to sort them out. Eventually the manager called Dad into his office one day and said,

"Well Keith we are sick of all the arguments and fights, we have decided to give you the sole right to take the breeze away."

With the stroke of a pen they had given Keith as he would say, "a license to print money". The material was his for free as long as he could cart it away. At the time Brisbane was going through a period of rapid development and "breeze" was in demand as solid fill for all kinds of earthworks and developments. Hundreds of suburban back yards were filled by O'Neill and Green and later O'Neill and Stabe, with their trucks being a common sight around Brisbane. On the north side of town schools such as Kedron and Hendra had thousands of cubic yards of breeze delivered by O'Neill's trucks. One day the Government overseer at the Hendra High School job got into an argument with the Old Man about not filling his trucks properly and that he was selling the Government short. Keith enjoyed telling the story about how he bamboozled the man by explaining the "angle of repose" and how to calculate volume.

Loading at the Gas Works. Photo O'Neill Collection

The company had an amazing list of clients and entries from their ledger in the early 1960's tell quite a tale. In February 1964 they had 57 separate deliveries totalling 2464 pounds 17 shillings and 8 pence. In December they had 31 deliveries totalling 1441 pounds 16 shillings and 7 pence. The list goes on. In November 1962, 3 clients paid for over 900 pounds each for "Breeze" and these were regular clients like the Main Roads department and Beavis & Bartells, a plumbing and construction company.

A quick look at Google reveals that a man's average wage for that time was 13 pounds 11 shillings a week. They were generating cash flow of approximately 25-30 times a man's wage. The later records have disappeared, but eventually they had several more trucks and were one of the first Brisbane companies to install two way radio's in their vehicles. Many were the stories I heard about trucks getting bogged in customers' back yards, old ladies complaining about their grass being wrecked, broken down trucks having to be towed home and drivers coming and going. Dad was a generous boss and for some years they had Christmas parties in the local hall, with presents for the kids and bonuses for the drivers. He had a lot of fun and a lot of money in those days.

Just after the war there were many opportunities for money to made in the earthmoving and transport industries. Two of Keith best mates from the time, Jerry Wearing and Les Thiess made their fortunes buy helping to develop Brisbane after the war, with all three taking advantage of leftover lend lease equipment, that the US army had left behind. There are stories of fighter planes and other equipment being pushed over the side of ships in Morten Bay and buried out the back of the aerodrome. Sites dotted around Brisbane where surplus army goods were dumped and historical relics can be found are listed on Peter Dun's Oz@War web site. Stuff is still being uncovered.

Hard work was complimented with good times. Keith was in peak fitness and "playin' two up" was his favourite past time. These were the post war years when he and his mates were just starting out in business. The Old Man was a great two up player, he would take a ten pound note and a one pound note to a game, if he lost that he would go home, but often he won.

"Did you hear about the time the cops were chasing us behind the Wynnum golf course? That was a bloody corker! Who did we take? Frank Wearing, he comes with me, OK. And we all got away from them, they were in their suits. Anyway, this one, we're playin' behind the golf club, in the scrub. I didn't like playin' in the scrub because you couldn't see them. If you played in the open you could see them and they could see you too. Anyway, there's a raid on and we're off! I said to this bloke, follow me! And I off, and it turns out there's a couple of senior coppers there in their suits, and they've got a bloody squad of what do ya call em? recruits, young blokes in sand shoes and socks that can run like a bloody hare, there chasing me and Frank's a yard behind me, we runnin' like hell and he's singin' out "Stop in the name of the King!"

I'm about a couple of yards in front of him and he's gaining on me and there's a three strand barbed wire fence in front of me, and I'm tryin' ta think, will I stop to crawl to get underneath it or will I clear it? Me brain's tickin' over and he's gaining on us, not very fast but he's gaining. So I said "Jump this Frank, follow me, jump this"!

"I don't know whether he heard me or not but I jumped it. I cleared it by a few inches and unknowns to me when I cleared it, I scraped the back of my hand on the top wire, I didn't realise it. He jumped it and he must have cleared it too. Well the copper stopped and by the time he got under the fence we were gone. When we stopped Frank said what happened to your hand? But it was only a little nick. Oh we had a ton of fun!"

"Other times we used to play under the old gum tree at Hendra. It was a great spot as it was out in the open and we had a cockatoo (a young boy) up the tree. If the coppers were coming the cockatoo would call out "GO!" and we would off. Any way one day we were playin' there and the call went out "GO". We grabbed our money and took off and ran towards the creek that was a few hundred yards away. A copper was after me calling out, "Stop in the Name of the King". When we got to the creek the copper was still following so I jumped in and waded across. He stopped on the bank and called out "Come back here you dingos."

We laughed and went up onto the bank of the far side. After he left I took the wet notes out of my pocket and dried them on the bank. The coppers used to be in heavy three piece suits and boots. They would be knocked up after about fifty meters. But we always played in shorts and bare feet. Often it was a hot day and we kept a kerosene tin of water for drinking. One day we were on the run from the coppers and we heard a few gun shots, I got a bit of a spurt on. Later we found our water tin had four bullet holes in it."

"We had only been playin' in a paddock, when later on a bloke said to us,
"How would you like to go to a big game, where there's no coins?"
"What do you mean by that - no Coins?
He said "Dice and there's a minimum limit on what you can bet."
So I went there, and I got a hell of a run on, I couldn't go wrong! I was backing a tail all the time. Couldn't go wrong! And I'm winning heaps of bloody money. I thought this is bloody good! So I said to the ring keeper,
"When can I go?"
He said "You can go whenever you like."
So I thought the idea was to go when I'm in front. I had tenners - ten pound notes. Well I won a heap of bloody money and I thought I'm not gonna catch a tram home, I'll get a cab. I got a cab home and when I got to Ascot the cabbie said "Fourteen and sixpence or something." "Ah I said here's a fiver, good luck to ya."
He said "Oh whenever you want a lift home you get my number, I'll give you a lift home."

"Three hundred and thirty four quid I won that night. And I went back. I only played on a Sunday night, a properly conducted game.

And there was an ex fighter on the door and If you were drunk or looked like you were on the booze you wouldn't get in. If anyone won big money, nobody was allowed to leave for half an hour. You got half an hour's start to make sure that nobody's gonna knock you down."

The next episode seems straight out of a Keystone Cops comedy. How times have changed.

"There used to lots of games and we all got landed one night! The game was in a big hotel almost opposite the Customs house, a big flash hotel. And we didn't know that one of the night porters was running it. This night Don Green came with me. We all had dud names, you gotta stick to the same name, My was John Cyril Thomas. Well, we all got caught, this was 1948. How I know it was 1948, the new Holdens were just out and we all got rides in the new Holdens, when we were taken to the watch-house.

Did I tell you about the time we had a game there? "We all got caught and this copper only had three cars and there was a heap of us. Merv Gorrie - he's the leader of the police gang, he said," Now listen you bloody mugs, I can't get yas all in, he said" I've only got three cars, but It's only a matter of ringing up to get a council bus to get yas all in. But by that time it'll be after midnight and we get no overtime after midnight, so I've gotta have yas in and processed before midnight. Now here's what were gonna do." So he says,

"Hands up those that have got cars? I put my hand up." Now we're all gonna form a queue and your gonna go on trust. And he said "I know yas all and if ya don't all arrive at the watch house I'll be after yas!"

I had a second hand twin spinner, not very old, oh my pride and bloody joy. Twin spinner was the Customline Sedan, and I had that see. So he gets in my car. He said "I'll go in your car!" He got in the front with me, we never spoke about two up." "Gee this is a nice car to ride in. It's a beauty!" "He's talking like this, I felt like sayin' to him do you want a drive?"

"Anyhow we all get up there and were in the watch house. And he comes to us and says "We're gonna be late, there's a heap of bloody burglars and drunks and everything, were gonna be hours before ya get processed!" He says "What say I give ya the coins and ya have a game while were waitin'?"

"So we have a bloody game, and were just playin' in the bloody watch house. Were locked up, he took the bracelets off us and we're playin' there, we must have played for about an hour just as if we're outside playin'. What ya got was, ya forfeited a fiver bail, or you appeared the next morning and you got two quid back. And some did, not a lot, but some "

The Old Man reckons he had his first game of two up when he was about fifteen. They were carefree and the police had a more generous attitude towards such harmless illegal fun, in those days. However after the police acquired two way radios having a game became more difficult and they had to move around more. Eventually the Fitzgerald Inquiry into police corruption in Queensland put paid to the old ways.

CONCLUSION: THE END OF AN ERA

Before Keith got married, he bought a piece of sloping land on the edge of town at Toombul, near Schultz's canal, within sight of where he and his mates used to play two up in Wagner's Paddock. You can still see the old gum tree out in the open near the Hendra High School. It must have been a great memory standing in the back yard looking down on his former two up spot. He filled the land to level with breeze using his own trucks and tractors.

Filling the land Toombul, mid 1950's. O'Neill Collection

Having paid cash for a beautiful house to be built, he went on a honeymoon. Later some visiting American sailors dubbed it "The White House." Keith got married in 1955 and after a while he started to settle down into family life.

**Cyril Smith's Model T At the White House
Photo O'Neill collection**

In those days after the war American ships would frequent Brisbane for R&R, pulling up at Brett's Wharf. Being a passionate believer in all things American, he would link up with some sailors go out and "have a few" or "bend the elbow", reminiscing about the good old days no doubt. In the days before pokies "two up" was still commonly played in the 1950's. One night he got home late and his wife Meg asked:
"How did you go?"
"Oh I got about a thousand."
"What?' she said, "Lets count it now."

So at one a clock in the morning, they counted the cash on the kitchen table. Eleven hundred pounds, was a lot of money in 1956. They used the money to have some classic 1950's furniture made for the house, but this was one of the last of the Old Man's escapades. Soon children came along, the business boomed, he joined the local Lions and golf clubs and became a prosperous middle class business man. With two new cars parked in front of the White House it was quite a transformation, for a boy who had grown up selling sparrows, to pay the electricity bill.

Walkers Way, as it was called was the only street in Brisbane called a "Way". At one end was Wagner's farm house and across the creek was Wagner's paddock. In the 1960's, occasionally we would come home from holidays to find a flock of sheep in the front yard. Today you can still see the two up tree from the back yard but the view is different. Westfield built "The Big T", Toombul Shopping Town when I was about seven. Before that we kids used to play in the bush and catch guppies in the creek. Now instead of the creek and open grass land with a few trees, the "Airtrain" elevated rail line cuts the view and a tunnel takes traffic to the airport. Eagle Farm is not far away and instead of the dirt track we used to drive down, there is the biggest flyover in Queensland. The landscape and society of the 1940's has disappeared almost without trace. The family demolished the White House to make way for town houses but the trees Dad planted are still there. At the end of the street is the old Nundah cemetery with the graves of the pioneering German farmers not far from site of the Aboriginal settlement from the days of Tom Petrie. The Old Man passed away a couple of years ago and he is with his Mum and Dad.

And what of Pee Wee, and the 2/15th battalion? What is remarkable is how Jim maintained his friendships, family connections and great spirit in spite of all the hardships he had faced and the many battles won and lost against, fascists, poverty, loneliness and ill health.

Jim Sedawie, After the war. Photo O'Neill Collection

He rests in the Military section of the Lutwyche Cemetery in Brisbane, not far from the O'Neill plot. I never met Jim, he died in 1961 when I was 2. That he was sadly missed is conveyed by a fragment Keith kept from the funeral notices of the day, The Brisbane Telegraph 15 of February 1961.

"Sedawie, James George (Darkey Jim). The family of James Sedawie wish to THANK friends and neighbours for their floral tributes, cards telegrams and personal messages of sympathy in the recent loss of their dear and wonderful brother. Special thanks to Mr. & Mrs. W.K O'Neill, Mrs Glad Storey, the members of the RSL and the boys of the corner. As cards were too numerous and many address unknown, would all please accept this as a personal expression of gratitude."

There are not many of the original Battalion members still with us. However the 2/15th Remembrance Club has lots of active members. They carry the banner on Anzac Day, and proudly remember their fathers and grandfathers. Gordon and Jack who both fought all the way from North Africa to New Guinea and Borneo still remember the likes of Pee Wee, their mateship, and the deeds they were called to do.

Compiling this story has been a way of honouring their memory and keeping alive the values and culture they embodied. I have asked myself why write a book about war, the most unlikely of topics for me. But the story came to me and I felt compelled to write it out. It has given me some perspective on how fortunate I am to live in Australia at this time. After Anzac day this year I was reading an article in the Australian newspaper by Angela Shanahan. Some of what she said captures why this story is important. She remarks on the importance of history in understanding ourselves as a nation and society. What has happened to us and what Australians have done. As she said about the Australian War Memorial:

"One of the reasons for the last post ceremony is to tell an individual story everyday. These need to be told to young people especially.

They like it because it gives them a sense of meaning, belonging and purpose and emphasises values they find attractive within military history. Not with any affinity for wars - on the contrary- but more the values that come out of it."[1]

It is my hope that this work will find it's way into the hands of young people and be accessible and inspiring to them.

BIBLIOGRAPHY: TEXTS

Austin, Ron
Let Enemies Beware, The History of the 2/15th Battalion, 1940-45
Slouch hat Publications, Mc Crae, Aust 1995

Australian National Archives
Service Record. James George Sedawie, QX8724.

Australian Government, Dept. Of Veterans affairs,
North Africa and Syria: Australians in World War 2
Canberra, 2012

Byrnes, Mathew
Wartime Recollections: Australia Remembers 1945-1995 Published by. Motren Commemorative Committee
PO. Box. 207 Moorooka Brisbane, 4105
3217 1700

Caddick-Adams, Peter
Monty & Rommel, Parallel Lives.
Arrow, 2012, London

Charlton, Peter
South Queensland WW 2 1941-45
Boolarong Publications 1991
12 Brookes St Bowen Hills.

Collier R.
The War in the Desert. 1977 Time Life Books

Fitzsimons, Peter
Tobruk, Harper Collins, Australia, 2006.

Gammage, Bill
The Biggest Estate on Earth, How Aborigines Made Australia, Allen & Unwin Australia, 2011

Jones, David & Nunan, Peter
Subs Down Under, Brisbane 1942-1945
Boolarong Press Brisbane 2011

Lee Kuan Yew
The Singapore Story, Singapore Press Holdings, 1998

MacKenzie-Smith, John
Tobruk's Easter Battle, The Forgotten Fifteenth's date with Rommel's Champion
Boolarong, Brisbane, 2011.

Mc Donald
Damien Parer's War.
Lothian Books, 2003

McMaster, Hugh
The Brisbane Line, self published, Central Qld. Uni Press.

Marks Roger R
Queensland Airfields WW2 - 50 Years On
Pub. R & J Marks, 1994
20 Koumala St. Mansfield Brisbane. Q. 4122
page.

Macintyre, Stuart, *A Concise History of Australia* (Melbourne: Cambridge Univ Press, 2004

Monteath Peter
POW, Australian Prisoners of War in Hitler's Reich
Macmillian Aust. 2011

Motren Commemorative Committee Wartime Recollections: Australia Remembers 1945-1995

Petrie, Constance Campbell
Tom Petrie's Reminiscences of Early Queensland,
Watson Ferguson Brisbane, 1904

Pott.D & Potts A.
Yanks Down Under 41-45
The American Impact on Australia
Oxford Uni Press. Melbourne, 1985.

Smith, Graham
Shadows of War, On the Brisbane Line, Boolarong Press Brisbane 2011

Stanley, Peter
Invading Australia, Japan and the Battle for Australia,1942
Viking, Penguin Australia, 2008

Swanston & Swanton, Murdoch Press, Australia, 2010
The Historical Atlas of World War 2.

Thompson, Peter A and Macklin, Robert, The Battle of Brisbane. ABC Books 2000,

Wilmot, Chester Tobruk 1941
First Published Halstead Press, Viking Books, Penguin Group. London. 1944, Later Edition. Penguin Australia. 2007 250 Camberwell road Camberwell 3124

1. **Web Sites.**

http://home.st.net.au/~dunn/civilian/allisontestingarea.htm

Rudd Bill: Free Men of Europe, http://www.aifpow.com/

Brisbane Living Hertiage.org, self guided tour for Brisbane Wartime History.

History of Stalag 18A
http://www.stalag18a.org.uk/history18a.html

Pegasus Archive
http://www.pegasusarchive.org/pow/

Record of Subs in Brisbane
http://home.st.net.au/~dunn/locations/sthbnedrydock.htm

2. **Interviews.**

    1. Sgt. Gordon Wallace. Brisbane 2012, Member 2/15th battalion, President B Coy, 2/15th Battalion
    2. Sgt. Jack Anning, 2012. Brisbane. Member A Coy, 2/15th Battalion

Alison Flaherty. Nee Harding Buderim. Brisbane resident, 1940's.

Keith O'Neill, Brisbane resident, 1922-2010. Recorded oral history 1996-2000.

3. **Documents.**

James George Sedawie, QX8724, Brisbane resident, 1903-1961. member 2/15th Battalion. War correspondence.

Keith O'Neill, Collected ephemera, including official documents, newspaper cuttings and photos

APPENDIX. 1

The Sayings of W.K. O'Neill (abridged version)

1. Greetings and Salutations from W.K. O'Neill and how the bloody hell are ya?

2. He's been around since Adam played fullback for Hamilton

3. He's been around since Adam had shorts

4. See you round the fridges.

5. A bird in the hand is worth two in the bush

6. He's spitting chips

7. He's dragging the chain

8. Slow as a wet week

9. Great minds think alike, fools never differ

10. Your too smart for this world you ought to be up with the astronauts

11. Getting an ear bashing

12. Having a chin wag

13. Two heads are better than one

14. He's got an old head on young shoulders

15. He doesn't know whether he punched or borred

16. Two wrongs don't make a right

17. Don't let the right hand know what the left hand is doing

18. Keeping a poker face

19. Play your cards close to your chest

20. It's raining cats and dogs

21. Worse things happen at sea

22. Standing around like a house to let

23. Don't scratch your head you'll get splinters

24. A lick and a promise

25. No skin off your teeth

26. Running on all cylinders

27. Don't try to pull the wool over my eyes

28. Grin and Bear it

29. I believe you thousands wouldn't

30. Give you the benefit of the doubt

31. It'll be on for young and old

32. I'll cross that bridge when I come to it

33. There's more to it than meets the eye

34. We're all in the same boat

35. Your treading on dangerous ground

36. Your skating on thin ice

37. Don't frighten the horses

38. I'll wipe that smile off your face

39. You're a better man than me Gungadin

40. There's always two sides to a story

41. You learn a lesson every day of your life

42. You think I came down with the last shower

43. The brain box is ticking over

44. When the penny dropped

45. Not tonight Josephine

46. All I want for Christmas is me two front teeth

47. Charges like a wounded bull

48. Never underestimate the power of a kind word or deed

49. Don't cut off your nose to spite your face

50. Don't put the cart before the horse

51. That's water under the bridge

52. Passed with flying colours

53. Let's hit the dusty trail

54. You have a short fuse

55. Patience is a virtue

56. That's the $64 question

57. You've got Buckley's

58. Throw you in the deep end

59. Wouldn't be dead for quids

60. Sticks out like a sore thumb

61. He's not short of a quid

62. I've got a bone to pick with you

63. Like a pig in mud

64. Shut that door, do you think I live in a tent

65. Put your thinking cap on

66. Sticks and stones will break my bones but names will never hurt me

67. Any old tick of the clock

68. Throw a spanner in the works

69. Water off a ducks back

70. Talk under wet cement

71. Holy suffering catfish

72. You don't have to be Einstein to work that out

73. That's not enough to fill my hollow tooth.

74. Ask a silly question and you'll get a silly answer

75. Your guess is as good as mine

76. Keep it under your hat

77. Your blood's worth bottling, for the pigs

78. Beggars can't be choosers

79. You can lead a horse to water but you can't make him drink

80. We're not out of the woods yet

81. You are on you Pat Malone

82. Give him a wide berth

83. Keep him at arms length

84. Tarred with the one brush

85. Ya nong

86. My pocket thinks my hand has gone mad from diving into it

87. Money burns a hole in your pocket

88. He's in more trouble than Flash Gordon

Songs for long car trips

Don't fence me in.

Give me land lots of land neath the starry skies above,
Don't fence me in
Let me ride through the wide open country that I love
Don't fence me in.

Let me be buy myself in the evening breeze,
Listen to the murmer of the cotton wood trees,
Send me off forever but I ask you please
Don't fence me in

I want to ride to the ridge where the west commences,
Gaze at the moon till I lose my senses
I can't look at hobbles
And I can't stand fences
Don't fence me in

Comin Round the Mountain

She'll be comin round the mountain when she comes
She'll be comin round the mountain when she comes

She'll be riding 6 white horses when she comes,
She'll be riding 6 white horses when she comes,

She'll be wearing pink pajamas when she comes,
She'll be wearing pink pajamas when she comes,

It's a long way to Tipperary

It's a long way to Tipperary
It's a long way to go,
Goodbye Piccadilly
Farewell Leicester Square,
It's a long way to Tipperary
But my heart's right there.

Bless Em All

They say there's a troop ship just leaving Bombay
Bound for old Blimey's shores
Heavily laden with time expired men,
Bound for the land they adore,

There's many an Ensign just finishing his time,
Many a twerp signing on,
You'll get no promotion this side of the ocean,
So cheer up my lads bless em all,

Bless em all, bless em all,
The long and the short and the tall,
Bless all the sergeants and WO1's,
Bless all the corporals and their blinkin' sons,
For we're saying goodbye to them all,
And back to their billets they crawl,

You'll get no promotion this side of the ocean,
So cheer up my lads bless em all

Kiss me Goonight

Kiss me good night sergeant major'
Tuck me in my little wooden bed,
We all love you Sergeant major
When we hear you calling "show a leg",

Don't forget to wake me in the morning
And bring me round a nice hot cup of tea
Cor Blimey
We all love you sergeant Major
Sergeant major be a mother to me, oi !

Roll out the Barrel, (extract)

Roll out the barrel, we'll have a barrel of fun
Roll out the barrel, we've got the blues on the run
Zing boom tararrel, sing out a song of good cheer
Now's the time to roll the barrel, cause the gang's all here!

Show me the Way TO Go Home

Show me the Way TO Go Home

I'm tired and I want to go to bed

I had a little drink about an hour ago

And it's gone right to my head

ABOUT THE AUTHOR

Mark O'Neill grew up in Brisbane during the 1960's when the "city" was like a big country town. Disappearing for hours to play in the creek and bush, with friends, he developed a fondness for open space and freedom. The creek would flood every year and in 74 it went over the houses near the canal. As luck would have it his Dad has created an oasis on top of land filled above the flood. A spirit of independence was passed on to him as the "Old Man" would tell stories of Brisbane in the early days, before rock and roll and when being called a "old bastard" was still a term of endearment. The fun and carefree episodes stuck a cord and eventually they were recorded and copied down, the end result being this book. Keith O'Neill was a great story teller and Mark hopes this trait will stay in the family. The Author has his own son's now and is enjoying passing down what it means "when Adam had shorts" and "if you scratch your head you'll get splinters."

APPENDIX 2. LETTER 1.

Qx8724 Pte. J. Sedawie
2/15th Bat
A Coy
A.I.F Abroad
17/8/1941

Dear Keith,

Your ever welcome letter to hand today and was pleased to hear from you as yours was a lucky letter, as they sank our mail in the harbor and yours was one of the few saved. You have no idea how hard it is form them to get mail to us. You know where we are fighting and that is all we hold, we are holding the town and the harbor and the Huns are a half moon around us, but I think we have just about got the upper hand of him now and by xmas I hope to be out here, you were asking me about close shaves, well no person is safe in Tobruk no matter where he is as our furtherest point from the sea is about seven miles, and what damage their guns cannot do their dive bombers can do, and believe me you have no idea how them dive bombers make you get under cover,

We have him frighten at night time because we sneak up on him at different places and always clean up a few of them, they are that frighten now that they have a searchlight, but that does not stop us and as for the Italians they are the frighterest men I have ever come across. They have watch dogs, and believe me once the dog arks, we can start chasing them but can never catch up to them, they have had the best of equipment, we are still using their big guns against them…..

I am going to send you a couple of souvenirs and a couple of helmets. I will also send you two big shells which you can make into pint pots, the officer came round the other day and took all the field glasses and revolvers off the boys, but I still have your rifle.

About them smokes for the sick soldiers, I believe the boys who are wounded in the hospitals get all the cigarets they need, of course they are not left here, they are taken away to Alexandria 300 miles away, we are still on 50 cigarets a week, and they often miss out, we would have to go without smokes at times, only we go out and raid the Huns and take their tobacco off them.

Well Keith I was pleased to know that you are working and getting good money and see if you can hang on there till I get back and then you and I will go in for some sort of business, I wish you were just finishing the bat that was going to bring me back to Auzzie, as this place is making an old man of me, all the young fellows are just nervous wreaks, as you have no idea the affect the dive bombers have on us, especially when about 50 or 60 come diving down on you, and if a bomb drops close you go deaf for a week, and each plane carries 5 bombs and then they machine gun us, so you can imagine how our nerves are when they come round 14 or 15 times a day.

I have known a time when I haven't left my trench for 3 days, only to have a few shots when I could not hear a plane about, we have no air force to protect us, so we just have to take it as it comes. Every one of their infantry men carry a machine gun of some description while we have 1 to every 7 men, and still we can beat them, they are terrible frighten of our bayonets. One German officer we shot the other day, said before he died, said, it is not war with you Australians the way you keep advancing on us under such heavy machine gun fire. 30 of us took 120 prisoners and they took us by surprise as were advancing in the open, and they were in trenches, but we never stopped.

Well Keith I want you to send me a few things, I want you to send me a writing pad a 6 packets of envelopes and also 6 hack saw blades and 3 small flat files and I will make you some souvenirs…….

Well Keith this is about all the news for the present, so I will close wit heaps of luck hoping to hear from you by return mail.

Yours truly

Jim

APPENDIX 2. EXTRACT FORM LETTER LETTER 2.

14-10-41
QX 8724
PK. J Sedawie

Dear Keith,

Your ever welcome letter to hand today, and I am pleased to hear that you are still working and everybody is ok at home. Remember me to Pommy and tell him that by the time you get this letter I will be with him and expect to have xmas dinner with him. I thought would have left Tobruk 4 or 5 days ago, but I am still here, things have been pretty hot here these last few nights there have been a few deadly battles, that may have been the reason we have been left here. I am just dying to get out of here and and have a dam good feed of fresh meat and eggs and things, and have a good hot bath and clean up. Well Keith don't ask me any more news about things we do here, as we have a new officer, and this will be my first lot of letters to him, and if he reads them I will not be able to say too much, anyhow

p. 2

I will soon find out, and if he does the same as our last officer you just sign the envelope well I can tell you anything. There has been a boat load of parcels leave Tobruk 4 days ago, so I suppose your parcels have only just left, I have sent you about a dozen parcels, all war souvenirs I also sent you the rifle and ammunition and I forgot to tell you in my last letter, but it is too late now, that I got 4 hacksaw blades and about 7 files out of a German tank which we blew up. I Made a few rings, I broke all the blades as I do not have a handle for them, but as soon as I get out of Tobruk I will send you a piece of German propeller, and you can make a few rings, it will be easier for you to make them than me, because it took me a week too make each hole, as I had to start off with only a knife point, until the hole was big enough for the file. The stuff the propellers are made of is Geralium it is as light as Aluminum and as hard as steel.

NOTES TO CHAPTERS

1. Ascot
1. http://en.wikipedia.org/wiki/Brisbane_River
2. Petrie 16.
3. http://queenslandplaces.com.au/node/124
4. Gammage 152
5. Gammage 254
6. Petrie p.4
7. Petrie 184
8. http://www.brisbaneqld.com.au/ascot/history.html
9. Petrie 2

2. Fun & Games
1. Stuart Macintyre, A Concise History of Australia (Melbourne: Cambridge Univ Press, 2004), p. 178.
2. http://www.library.uq.edu.au/fryer/brisbane_btw/page7.html.

3. Tobruk North Africa, 1941
1. Austin 12
2. Collier. 32.
3. Collier. 32.
4. McDonald 125.
5. Wilmot, 99.
6. Caddic-Adams 253
7. Caddic-Adams 256
8. Austin P.57
9. Interview Mackenzie-Smith 2010

10. Austin 60
11. Wilmot p99
12. Jack Anning Interview 1012
13. James Sedawie Letter April 1941
14. Mackenzie- Smith 51
15. Austin 98.
16. Wilmot 130
17. Austin 79
18. Dept Veterans Affairs 126
19. Austin 85
20. Wilmot 255
21. McDonald 145
22. Australian War Memorial, extract the Official war diary, 2/15th battalion
23. North Africa & Syria, Dept Veterans Affairs 22

4. The War Comes to Ascot
1. Charlton, Peter, Page 8.
2. Charlton, Page 31
3. http://trove.nla.gov.au/newspaper, Courier Mail 1Feb 1947
4. Lee Kuan Yew, p52
5. Byrnes, Mathew, p47
6. Interview Alison Flaherty (Nee Harding) 2012.
7. Brisbane Heritage Living p 6.
8. Byrnes, Mathew, p15
9. http://trove.nla.gov.au/newspaper, Courier Mmail 18/2/45
10. Stanley, Peter Invading Australia,140

5. The Endless Patrol, Palestine & Syria
1. Austin 114

6. ElAmien & the Battle for Pee Wee Ridge
1. Austin 132.
2. James Sedawie letters.1941.
3. Austin 132
4. Jack Anning Interview 2102

5. Austin 139.
6. Austin151.
7. Caddic-Adams, 158

7. POW.
1. MacKenzie-Smith 100
2. Gilbertson 5
3. http://www.aifpow.com/part_1__missing_in_action,_believed_pow/chapter_4__transportation_of_pow/a._by_sea
4. Rudd Bill : Website: Ted Faulks in POW Free Men in Europe,
5. Knott, Gilbert http://www.pegasusarchive.org/pow/gilbert_knott.htm
6. Monteath 115.
7. Monteath117
8. History of s18a http://www.stalag18a.org.uk
9. Austin 189
10. Monteath 185.
11. Austin 189
12. http://www.stalag18a.org.uk
13. Monteath 392.
14. http://www.stalag18a.org.uk/history18a.html
15. Monteah 412
16. Service Record James Geroge Sedawie
17. Service Record James Geroge Sedawie

8. The Real Invasion
1. Charlton, Peter, p28
2. http://trove.nla.gov.au/newspaper, Courier Mail 1Feb 1947
3. Potts & Potts p. 132.
4. Thompson & Macklin, p. 102
5. Potts & Potts, P. 166
6. Charlton, Peter, p 28
7. Thompson & Macklin, p. 99
8. Charlton, Peter, p. 27
9. http://trove.nla.gov.au/newspaper, Courier Mail June 22 1942.
10. Charlton, Peter, p. 24.

9. Kangaroo Point
1. Jones, D & Nunn P. P.137

10. The Battle of Brisbane
1. Charlton, Peter, p. 26
2. Thompson & Macklin, p. 211
3. http://trove.nla.gov.au/newspaper, Courier Mail 27/11/42
4. Thompson & Macklin, p 212.
5. http://trove.nla.gov.au/newspaper, Courier Mail 27/11/42
6. Thompson & Macklin, p 215
7. Potts. D & Potts A. P 305.
8. Stanley, Peter p. 171

11. Keep the War Quiet: Eagle Farm
1. http://www.ozatwar.com/civilian/allisonigloos.htm
2. http://www.ozatwar.com/rofqld.htm
3. http://en.wikipedia.org/wiki/Martin_B-26_Marauder.
4. http://trove.nla.gov.au/newspaper, Courier Mail 1Feb 1947
5. Queensland Airfields WW2 - 50 Years On, p149

INDEX

A
Aborigines, 1, 3,4
Americans, 57,-61, 80-81,103,107-114,126,129,133,137-140
Africa 88, 91
Alexandria 31, 34,45,55,71, Appendix 2
Albacore 123

B
Brawls 108,111-115,131-133,
Breakfast Creek xii, 5, 9, 54, 67, 113, 123,
Brett's Wharf 58
Bulimba, 6,144, Operation, 89-90,95
Blamey, General, 31-32, 81,
Breeze 151, 153, 158.

C
Churchill, Winston 29-31, 63, 76,79-81,98
Curtin, John, xv, 63, 75-76, 81,
Cunningham, Allan, 3-4
Cunningham, Long John, 43, 73, 85-86, 93
Cockatoo 154
Chamberlin, Neville, Xiii
Coppers 22, 155, 154

D
Darwin, 27, 28, 63, 66, 68, 134
Depression, xx 111, 11, 13,18,42,79,111,145

Dive Bomber 45, 81, 125, Apex. 2,
Dry Dock, 116, 118,121-124,

E
Eagle Farm, x,111,1,3,5,6,59,107,126,135,136,141,145,149,160
Easter Battle, 36, 38, 48
El Alamein, 79, 81, 88, 91, 95,
Evans Deakin, 116, 119,122,124

F
Football, xiv, 50, 102,149,
Ford 6, 12,146
French 41,71,72,99,100,

G
Greece, 31,32,95,99
Growler, US Sub, 123
Grand Central Hotel, 109, 115,
Gruppignano, 96
Geneva Convention, 89, 99

H
Hitler 31, 78, 88, 91
Hamilton, xii,xv,1,3,5,7,13,23,55,107,125,135,144,149,

I
Italian, 29-31
Italy, 92, 95, 97, 104
Invasion, 63-68, 71-75,107,134

J
Japanese, xiii, xv, 57,61 ,63

K
Kitty Hawk, 137,141

L
Libya, 29, 30

M
Menzies, R, xiii, 31,
Montgomery, 75, 77-80, 89-91, 98
Morshead 37, 38, 39, 41, 46, 81,82,92
Marauder, 125,136,139
MacArthur, 57,109,
Marlan, Col. Spike, 27,33, 34
Mussolini, 28,30,31,94,
Mera Berga,35,

N
Newstead, 19, 67, 146, 15
9th Division, xiv , 31,37,69, 74,-,79,98,91,98
Negros, 109,110

P
Petrie. Tom, 3, 2,4, 160
Ponath, G , 42,
Polish, 41,56,
Parer, Damien, 45, 54,128
Prostitutes, 110-113
Palestine, 28,32,56,71
Provos, 109,115,128-130,132

R
Racecourse, vii, 5,7,14,
Rationing, xv, 12,144
Red Cross, 66, 96, 99-101,103,128
River Burdekin, 119
Riveting, 117
Rommel,31,33,35,37,39,45,47,50,55,77,79,88,91
Russians, 72, 98,100,102
Riot, 112,127,129-133

S
Salient, 49
Singapore, xiii, 63, 66, 75
Stalag xviii, 93
Story Bridge, 116,125
Stuka, 45-48, 54
Submarine, 66, 96,121,123, 59,116
Suez Canal, 27, 34-36, 77, 79

T
Tanks, 29, 39-41,48, 76,79,90
Test Stands, 135
Tobruk, viii, 29, 31, 33-37,41-55,77,83-86,96
Townsville,65 ,68,76
Trench, 36-38,41-43,47,49,51,67-68,82-83,177
Trocadero, 109
Trucks,23,32,35,56,59,95,100,104,117,146,148,151,153
Turrubal, xiii,5
Two Up, 21, 22,153,154,157,159,160

V
VDC, xiii,127,
W
Wolfsberg, 98
Watch House, 157

X
XXXX, xii, 150

www.ingramcontent.com/pod-product-compliance
Lightning Source LLC
Chambersburg PA
CBHW051125160426
43195CB00014B/2353